Oysters on the Half Shell

Historic Hotels of the Mother Lode

& the Recipes

That Make Them Famous

❧ 1849 ❧
❧ TO THE PRESENT ❧

Janet Irene Atkinson

Book Cover by Wendell Dowling

Editing, typesetting, layout and illustration refinements by
Graphics For Business

Special editing by Sharon Marovich.
Sonora, California 95370 U.S.A.

ISBN 0-9653428-4-0
Printed in the United States of America

Published by
Jan Irene Publications

P.O. Box 934
Sonora, California 95370 U.S.A.

Dedication

To good friends:

*Pat and Earl Williams, Chris Holman
Patty Wright, Melanie Jackson,
Carol Giordano, Sharon Marovich
and Alan Haack*

Table of Contents

List of Illustrations & Photos

Chef George Léger and his playmates
Painting (detail) courtesy of The Léger

Introduction

ow did *Oysters on the Half Shell* come to be? Two reasons. The first reason occurred at a book signing in Amador City, California. It was a beautiful day and I was signing books at the town's annual craft fair. The small community is about as quaint as a Mother Lode town can be— picture postcard perfect. A proverbial babbling brook flowed under an old bridge where my booth had been set up. Alongside the brook, there were rows upon rows of large overhanging shade trees and across the street, The Imperial Hotel was welcoming guests. Down the street were antique shops, the old jail, which houses the historical society and further down the sidewalk was the best— and I mean the best—bakery in all the Mother Lode: Andrae's Bakery and Cheese Shop. Amador City is only one block long, but of all the towns along the gold dust trail it is one of the most unique and inviting.

Next to me was a close friend whose booth featured nuts, dried fruit and dips. As the day wound down to the more quiet afternoon, I couldn't help but notice the number of people who con- sistently stopped by her booth for goodies.

"Why don't you put some kind of snack on your table?" she suggested. That idea did not particularly appeal to me, but the real- ization of the popularity of food products struck a chord which I could not forget. That was how the initial idea for *Oysters on the Half Shell* was born.

I wondered, for example, what the differences were between the tastes and menus of the 19th, 20th and 21st centuries. Today's Haute Cuisine has introduced a myriad of new tastes and foods from all over the world, sometimes in breathtaking combinations. But the reality is that the hotels and clientele of the Gold Rush were equally as cosmopolitan as are the hotels of today, perhaps even more so. The Gold Rush brought the world to the doorstep of the Mother Lode: Chinese, Chileans, Mexicans, Spanish, Italians, French and many more nationalities all came together, bringing their foods with them. Their tastes are reflected in the menus of the time.

Why the title *Oysters*? I believe it's because I associate oysters with elegant dining and gourmet taste. Oysters on the Half Shell was an item featured on the menus of all the better hotels during the Gold Rush. They were a mark of the excellence of the hotel, a kind of endorsement that advertised the area's up and coming status in the often snobbish and pretentious world of San Francisco. In comparison, the foothills of the Sierra seemed rather gauche and out of touch. Hotel owners were determined to change that image. Today, a large part of the clientele in the Mother Lode comes from the great city by the bay—indeed, many of their chefs as well.

The oyster, as a food item, has a long history. They were enjoyed by the Romans and eventually they spread throughout the empire. With the fall of Rome, they did not return until the Renaissance. Soon thereafter, they were so popular they were shipped around the world. By the 1900s, supplies waned due to overharvesting and disease. As a result wild oysters became rare and today supplies come from farm-raised varieties.

There is a legend that oysters are an aphrodisiac. The reasons are, as it turns out, based on fact. They are loaded with zinc and that helps keep testosterone levels normal. It was said that the famous womanizer Casanova ate fifty oysters every morning—nothing like being prepared for a lively night on the town!

There are more than 400 varieties of oysters, but today only three are popular. There is the small European flat oyster and the large American oyster found on our East and Gulf Coasts. And there are the large Japanese oysters now found in France and along the Pacific Coast of the United States.

With good food as my first reason, the second reason for writing the book was my love of architecture. When I first arrived in the Mother Lode, I was amazed to see how many 19th century hotels were still standing, still operating. Then, as fate would have it, I happened to drive by the St. George Hotel in Volcano and fell in love. The initial idea of indulging my love of food and my love of historical preservation and architecture merged— *Oysters On The Half Shell* was born.

I also wondered what the old hotels were like. A look at Angels Camp at the turn-of-the-20th-century turns up several hotels: the Angels Hotel, the What Cheer House, the Commercial Hotel, the Golden Eagle Hotel, Central Park Hotel, Hotel Southern and the Calaveras Hotel. The Calaveras Hotel was by far the largest, a three-story, fifty-room hotel. Each room had a bed, a dresser, wash stand, a pitcher and a chair. Baths were at the end of a long hall which opened onto porches. There was no heat in the rooms. When a meal was ready, someone would ring a dinner bell in the lobby, then go outside in the street and ring it again. Cooks were typically Chinese. Meals consisted of steak, chops, roast and a vegetable. There were three and four desserts, including pies. Price for room and board? Twenty-five dollars a month which included everything. My, oh my, how times have changed![1]

As I began writing, I was faced with the question of definitions. What is a hotel, an inn, a lodge, an auberge, a bed and breakfast, a saloon, tavern and a bar? Over the years, the words remain, but their usage has changed considerably. In the Old West, the word *hotel* was sometimes not even seen on a boarding establishment. *Webster's* defines an *inn* synonymously with that of a hotel. It is a place of shelter for lodging and entertainment of travelers—for compensation. *Auberge* is also the same word for an inn, but in French. Why it is seen in only a few inns is because owners may want to add an air of sophistication to their establishment, or wish to attract foreign guests. The word is associated more with bed and breakfast inns than hotels.

When we think of hotels today, we tend to think in terms of large chains like the Hilton and Hyatt, sometimes accommodating hundreds of people. Size, therefore, tends to separate inn from hotel. A *lodge,* on the other hand, is associated with a residence set apart for the hunting season or other special seasons. Sometimes it is a house on an estate occupied by a gamekeeper. Again, lodge is nevertheless seen on signs that have nothing whatsoever to do with hunting. I personally think of a lodge as relating to colder climates, like a ski lodge. A bed and breakfast inn on the other hand is usually

[1]Penelope Newton, Calaveras Hotel. Unpublished paper at the Calaveras County Historical Society, San Andreas.

a private residence that provides breakfast for guests. Of course, in Europe, you might find a bed and breakfast inn that is a magnificent castle, sitting amidst acres of well-manicured lawns. It may be large, but it is a private residence. In California "B&Bs" are generally small and seldom entertain more than four or six guests at one time. They are also much more personal than a hotel. Owners and guests are far more intimate, often meeting at dinner over a glass of wine, discussing the day's activities around a cozy fire.

A *saloon*, located in many of the hotels, was originally a place for men only, and catered to aristocratic gentlemen. Bars on the other hand were at the lower end of societal levels. They often opened earlier for those men who preferred to get their day started with a drink. Bars have risen in rank, however, becoming more sophisticated while saloons evoke sawdust floors and informality.

A *tavern* was originally designated for the retailing of liquors, but also accommodated overnight guests. Today, all these definitions have blurred. One might see both the words Inn and Hotel on the same sign and others may use Inn and B&B together.

Most of the hotels in the Mother Lode have undergone extensive renovation at the hands of dedicated owners intent on restoring them to their original state. These owners relish talking about their establishments, spinning a yarn or two and regaling their guests with the amenities of a colorful era many of us secretly wish to relive. Only in the Mother Lode are so many historic hotels still operating, still bewitching their modern day visitors with the memories of a world well worth retrieving.

My intention as *Oysters* took shape was to list every vintage hotel along historic Highway 49 beginning at Madera County in the south and ending at Vinton in Plumas County, the terminus of the Golden Chain Highway. There are a total of ten counties along Highway 49: Plumas, Sierra, Nevada, Placer, El Dorado, Amador, Calaveras, Tuolumne, Mariposa, and Madera. The task was simply too great. Since I planned to visit each hotel as well, it became doubtful that I could undertake such an ambitious project. The twenty-five hotels featured are divided into three geographic sections: the Southern, the Central and Northern Mother Lode areas. These include six counties: Madera, Mariposa, Tuolumne,

Calaveras, Amador and El Dorado. This is the famous gold trail that the argonauts followed as they harvested yellow specks of gold dust from Mother Earth. The Cary House Hotel, located in El Dorado County, became the furthest north I decided to venture. I chose to stop there largely because it was where the recipe, Hangtown Fry, originated.[2]

Then I hoped to list all the hotels which were originally built in the area, but no longer operating. This also proved to be impossible. There were, during the height of the Gold Rush, hundreds of hotels. Even in small communities, there might have been as many as twenty hotels. So, I pared that idea down to include only those hotels that were still in business and had an adjacent restaurant. Later, I had to amend even that as well. Some of the restaurants have disappeared over time and the hotels were so outstanding I could not justify leaving them out. The Cary House Hotel in Placerville is an example. It no longer has a restaurant, but the recipe for *Oysters on the Half Shell* originated there, so obviously it had to be included. The Gunn House in Sonora is another example. It had a restaurant until very recently. The Fallon House Hotel in Columbia has an ice cream parlor next door, but alas, no restaurant. It is currently owned by The City Hotel in Columbia and it has an excellent restaurant. The Royal Carriage Inn in Jamestown does not have a restaurant (though it serves breakfast) nor does the National Hotel in Jackson which serves only lunch in the bar.

Another exception I made was to include the Chateau du Sureau. It is not an historic hotel in terms of its age, but quite new. However, this five-star hotel and Erna's Elderberry House Restaurant are simply too spectacular to be omitted. The style of architecture is French Country and every room is reminiscent of a 17th or 18th century museum. Erna's Elderberry House Restaurant serves the very best cuisine in all of the Mother Lode and, indeed, ranks with the finest restaurants in California and, for that matter, the world. It is exemplary of the most luxurious accommodations as well.

I also wanted to at least mention the hotels that were still standing, but were no longer operating as hotels. This too was

---

[2]*See the last chapter on the Cary House Hotel.*

overly ambitious, so I listed a few that had been significant such as the Avery Hotel near Murphys. This hotel has been operating since the early 1850s and only recently closed as a hotel and restaurant. I chose to list it among the other hotels because it is still intact; it was an important stagecoach stop and is a rare architectural gem. Then there was the famous Angels Hotel in Angels Camp where Mark Twain was inspired to write his famous story of the *Jumping Frog of Calaveras County*. Upstairs there was, until very recently, a room set aside for that encounter between Twain and the frog, Dan'l Webster. Alas, it is now gone. Also there is the Willow Hotel in Jamestown which was built in 1862. After numerous fires, it lost its upper story in 1978 which contained the hotel. Today, it is solely a restaurant. The Black Bart Inn has operated since 1927 and was closed until quite recently. Only the restaurant and a modern annex in the rear are currently operating. There was so much history here, I chose to write a chapter about the hotel's past glory. Hopefully, the old hotel will open its doors again.

I've revised an historic map, the Golden Chain '49er Highway map which was originally printed in 1959 and updated only once, in 1963—until now. All the hotels are marked on the map (by number in tiny black squares) and the chapters contain "how to get there" directions. Each chapter gives a brief description of the hotel's history, a sketch of the people who have visited, stories about the hotel, resident ghosts and finally, a few of the chef's favorite recipes. Included are photos of the hotel as it appears today and, whenever possible, pictures of the original hotel.

Foremost, I wanted to inform and excite my readers about the existence of the Mother Lode's oldest, most enduring and charming, historic hotels. In an age of fast food and less than inspiring hotel chains, the reminders of the area's colorful past are exemplified in these statuesque survivors. Vacationers to our Golden Shores have stated again and again that they prefer to visit historic sites more than all of the theme parks put together. They want the "real" thing, to rub shoulders in the same hotels that hosted some of the most notorious men and women of the West. There, they can relax in a sumptuous 19th century four-poster bed that still soothes a weary traveler. When they stroll up to long, mirrored, mahogany bars upon floors that creak with the reminders of a bygone era, the hectic pace of the modern world fades.

What did I learn after my trek up and down the Mother Lode visiting these historic hotels? I was somewhat surprised at the number of incredible events the hotels provide. These hotels are no longer just places for overnight stays or dining. The Chateau du Sureau in Oakhurst, the Groveland Hotel in Groveland and the Hotel Jeffery in Coulterville, offer classes in cooking and wine appreciation. In addition, for lovers of fine food, there is the Chef's Holiday hosted by The Ahwahnee Hotel in Yosemite, now in its 22nd year, where the country's most celebrated chefs display their skills before an audience. Each session features a Meet the Chef reception, cooking demonstrations, a behind-the-scenes kitchen tour and a sumptuous five-course gala dinner.[3]

All these hotels provide a wide variety of excursions to Yosemite National Park, theater attractions, live plays, horseback riding, fishing and the list goes on. Their monthly agenda is sometimes a little breathtaking. During all the holidays, the hotels offer celebrations fit for royalty.

The world has changed considerably since the days of the '49ers. We can all reminisce when we look back at the slightly outrageous raucousness of that earlier era. Most of us harbor an envious desire to go back to those long ago days, when bars rang out with the tinny sound of a piano, "soiled doves" were draped over the balconies awaiting potential customers, and life hung on the turn of a card. Today, the brawls are missing, most of the girls are gone and there are no more (rarely?) fist fights or gun battles. But the hotels are still there and while none of us can have it all, we can still enjoy their hospitality, serving the finest food in the Mother Lode and let our imaginations make up for the rest.

I do have a final suggestion. When you decide to visit a hotel call the local Visitor's Bureau in the area. They have a list of upcoming events, and you can tie your visit to the hotel of your choice with lots of wonderful things to see and do as well.

So, dear reader, feast upon them: these architectural wonders

---

[3]For more information visit: www.yosemitepark.com

of our colorful past are a joy to behold, and taste the culinary delights they serve up every day in their dining rooms.

As a final note to my readers, I feel that is important that I mention that all possible precautions have been taken to ensure that the recipes in this book are accurate as provided by the various chefs. We believe that they are ready for your use and if followed carefully will give you the final outcome intended by these excellent chefs. We hold no responsibility for errors or omissions in these recipes.

Acknowledgments

To all the innkeepers, my special thanks. Each and every one of them interrupted their busy schedules to show me around, and spent a great deal of time telling me about their hotel's unique and special charms.

Thanks to the Tuolumne County Historical Society on Bradford Street in Sonora where I perused their archives in the History Center and found many wonderful stories and unusual recipes from the gold fields. Two of these old time recipes I have included. These are not necessarily dishes one would want to recreate, but they do lend themselves to the ambiance of that era. (See pages 65 and 71).

Thanks, as always, to the Tuolumne County Library on Greenley Road in Sonora and its entire staff. I could not write anything without assistance from: Verna Cabral-King, Joan Rutty and Keith Behymer.

I wish to thank Doris Fletcher, author of *Jamestown* and *Growing up in Jamestown,* for her help with hotels in that charming community. I asked her to take some pictures for me at the last minute. When she arrived she had been up the night before with her husband, who had been ill, but made her date in spite of not feeling up to par.

My thanks also to Dr. Linda Bissonnette, Columbia State Historic Park District's cultural specialist, for her help on the Fallon House in Columbia.

Also my thanks to Cate Culver of the San Andreas Historical Society for the afternoon we spent together discussing The Black Bart Inn and Motel in San Andreas.

I am most grateful to those businesses who have helped with the costs of producing this book, and especially to Preston and Maurine Hotchkis of Santa Barbara for their grant.

And last, to good friends to whom I chose to dedicate the book. They often accompanied me on my visits to the hotels and made the long drives much more lively.

And finally, what a special friend I have in Sharon Marovich, a local historian. She offered her services to edit *Oysters*. I counted on her sharp eye to catch errors in the text, her extensive historical background to make changes in historical facts, her knowledge of cooking and her positive suggestions. She is a treasure.

History of the Golden Chain '49er Map

When miners and later settlers came into the Mother Lode in the 1850s roads were crude and the old wagons that made those long, difficult trips into the area were not exactly comfortable, to say the least. When motor transportation improved, a North-South Road became necessary. In 1916, during World War I, Proposition Four was passed. It was labeled the "good roads initiative." Suddenly there were road associations appearing everywhere, backed by local Chambers of Commerce.

In 1919 the Mother Lode Highway Association was formed and it became known as the Golden Chain Council in 1950. Finally in 1959, it was labeled Highway 49. The map of the highly detailed, Golden Chain Council is typically known as the *'49er Map* and shows all the old communities along historic Highway 49.

Although the original map was updated only once in 1963 in order to include Interstate 5, my editor found that the map was too detailed to be readable on our small pages. So we simplified it to show mostly just the towns along Highway 49 that are mentioned in our book along with the appropriate highway to reach them.

Legend for the Map - See numbered squares

1	Chateau du Sureau	**14**	The City Hotel
2	Wawona Hotel	**15**	Murphys Historic Hotel
3	Ahwanhee Hotel	**16**	Avery Hotel
4	Hotel Jeffery	**17**	Dorrington Hotel
5	Groveland Hotel	**18**	Black Bart Inn & Motel
6	Charlotte Hotel	**19**	The Léger Hotel
7	Jametown Hotel	**20**	National Hotel (Jackson)
8	National Hotel (Jamestown)	**21**	St. George Hotel
9	The Willow Steakhouse	**22**	Volcano Union Inn
10	Royal Carriage Inn	**23**	American Exchange Hotel
11	Sonora (Days) Inn	**24**	The Imperial Hotel
12	The Gunn House	**25**	Cary House Hotel
13	The Fallon House		

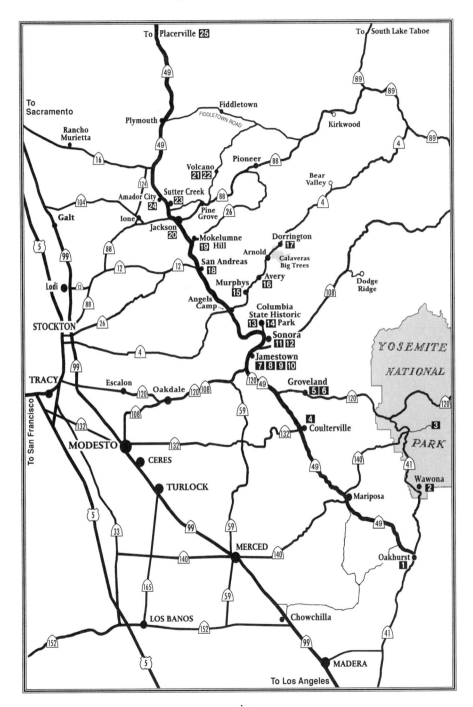

Dr. René Clanin and Erna Kubin-Clanin (center front) & staff – Chateau du Sureau

Chateau du Sureau 1991
Erna's Elderberry House 1984
OAKHURST

I have a suggestion. Before you visit the Chateau du Sureau, prepare yourself for a romantic trek into another dimension—a world where elegance, superb dining and beauty manage to keep the outside world at bay. Here is a true Renaissance magic kingdom created by a woman whose only goal is to make sure that her guests enjoy the finest haute cuisine in the West, and the most luxurious accommodations available anywhere.

Everyone has dreams. Many of us work very hard to see them realized and there are others who lose sight of their goals along life's sometimes uncertain twists and turns. Then there are those who seem quite literally *hitched to a star* and despite difficulties, never give up. These are the tenacious ones whose dreams may seem outlandish when measured against the possibility of success, but

1

who, nevertheless, persevere. This describes Erna Kubin-Clanin. She has managed to build a Five-Star restaurant, Erna's Elderberry Restaurant, which attracts lovers of fine food from all over the world. Her restaurant and palatial hotel, The Chateau du Sureau, and The Villa Sureau, are built on a nine-acre estate in the wilds of the Mother Lode! All of this draws clients who come from as far away as western Europe and Russia to experience the ultimate in superb dining and comfort.

Erna's magic carpet ride began in Vienna, Austria. Looking back on her journey one could not image a more ideal vision with which to begin. She had been surrounded by castles in her native land and raised on stories of kings, queens and fairy tales, but her journey was not sprinkled with stardust. Erna began humbly, working as a tea girl at the famous Claridge Hotel in London. Along the way she acquired a background in theater design, fine art and culinary skills. Crossing the "pond" in 1962, she came to our shores to receive a scholarship to the prestigious New York Academy of Art in Manhattan, and later completed her studies at the University of California Los Angeles (U.C.L.A.).

Once again, working at an up-scale restaurant in Redondo Beach, Erna began at the bottom. Into this caldron of creativity and masterful cooking, she added a lot of hard work and opened her own restaurant in Westwood, California—Scorpio's. Eight years later, emotionally and physically drained, she decided to pack her bags and move to a more tranquil setting—the central Sierra Nevada foothills.

Within months she leased the Redwood Inn close to the Wawona Hotel in Yosemite National Park. It seemed as if her fairy godmother had at last waved a magic wand over her aspiring young progeny. The restaurant was an enormous success and Erna filled it with the most beautiful paintings and furniture she could find, creating a warm, inviting home-like ambiance. Alas, in every fairy tale there is a villain. The culprit in this scenario turned out to be the national park system. Bureaucracy won out (for a while) over taste, art and beauty and Erna lost her lease.

Dreams, however, don't die easily for a young woman blessed with talent, brains and energy. She brushed aside her tears and resolved to begin again. Only this time, she would create her

2

own magic kingdom dependent upon no one but herself. In 1984 the impossible finally happened. Erna's Elderberry House rose on a nine-acre estate in the small town of Oakhurst. Here, Erna served as the chef until 1996. In that year, the restaurant became the highest rated Zagat[1] restaurant in America!

Dining establishments offering fare of this quality are typically located in major cities where there are art galleries, museums, high-end shopping and clientele who appreciate fine food and can afford the price tag. But beginning such an enterprise in a small rural town with a population of less than 20,000 people is daunting. The most upscale shopping in Oakhurst is at the local Sears department store and dining is somewhat limited to fast food take-out and cafes. In spite of this Erna's Elderberry House has attracted people from all over the world. One of these visitors was famed food writer Craig Claiborne of *The New York Times*, who had heard about Erna's restaurant and flew west in 1986 to see for himself if the accolades were true. He spent an enchanted three days in Erna's kitchen, cooking and enjoying her creations. When he mentioned the fact that accommodations were somewhat sparse in the area, Erna immediately envisioned yet another dream—a place to equal the superb caliber of her dining. In 1991 the ten-room Chateau du Sureau was ready for its first guest.

Erna's accomplishments have resulted in many culinary awards. She is a member of the prestigious Relais & Chateaux Hotel Association, winning the coveted Mobil Five-Star Award and Triple A Five-Diamond Award for thirteen years. These awards are given to fewer than twenty-five gourmet establishments in the United States and Canada. This is praise enough, but when one considers where the Chateau is located, it is nothing short of a miracle.

After receiving a beautiful packet of literature on the Chateau, complete with lavender silk ribbon and a silver-embossed brochure, I was curious to see for myself if such a unique phenomenon could actually exist in this somewhat remote corner of California.

From Sonora, I took Highway 49 to Mariposa and continued south to Oakhurst. I turned onto Highway 41 and immediately spied large iron oval-shaped gates to my right. The driveway, which

[1]zagat.com—Ratings and Reviews for over 25,000 of the world's best restaurants, nightspots, hotels and attractions

wound its way up to an impressive entrance, reminded me of an enchanted castle in Europe. I was enticed by the romantic hillside surrounded by beautiful old shade trees and lots of Elderberry bushes—hence the name Sureau, French for Elderberry.

The day I visited, I was greeted by a member of the Chateau's beautifully groomed staff who graciously welcomed me—manners sorely missing in today's culture. Walking into the front entrance, I felt as if I were entering a private home richly-furnished with beautiful old world antiques. Persian rugs covered the floor, magnificent tapestries and artwork adorned the richly-carved walls. A grand stairway embellished with antique tiles drew my attention as did the seventy-seat restaurant with hand-stenciled, beamed cathedral ceiling and three gorgeous brass chandeliers. The tables were

immaculately covered with white linen ablaze with fresh flowers from the garden and glistening crystal—a feast for the eyes.

A short time later, I was introduced to Daniel, the Chateau's full-time butler, who showed me into the main salon, or living room of the hotel. The salon was not only beautiful, but also welcoming. A crackling fire blazed in a large brick fireplace. There was a step-up three-tiered floor in one corner where an impressive baby grand piano resided, and outside the windows, a magnificent view of mountains, trees and gardens. Against one wall was a library furnished with high-back, commodious chairs, period paintings, and a large French armoire. Hidden away behind intricately carved cabinets were the necessary accouterments of our information age: a fax, computer and television.

My first impression was an overwhelming desire to sink down in one of the large chairs and never leave, but Daniel beckoned me to continue my tour. I was escorted along a swimming pool, a koi pond, and one by one, five luxurious bedrooms with massive French doors. Each had its own story to tell and most are named after local herbs—Chamomile, Rosehip, Mint, Saffron and Elderberry. Many of the rooms have their own fireplace; some have seductive uphol-stered nooks for writing letters (almost a lost art). Others have painted glass windows, displaying romantic scenes from a Medieval legendary tale of old. All have large, king-size antique beds pur-chased from auctions and estates all over Europe. The beds are sumptuously clad in silk comforters. Some were canopied, others richly draped to enclose the bed, if guests so desire. The bathrooms are reminiscent of tiled Roman baths with sunken tubs, double sinks and large tiled showers. Each bath contained an assortment of exqui-site bath powders, and every possible convenience the Chateau's fortunate guests could desire. When a guest rises in the morning after sleeping on Lisa Galimberti's luxurious Italian sheets, a maid is dispatched to plump the pillows. Upon returning to their room, guests might also find a sachet tied with ribbons, filed with an assortment of freshly-baked, delectable cookies.

Walking back to the salon, Daniel opened yet another door and another surprise: a small chapel. Next to the chapel was an intimate dining room and fireplace which seats up to twelve. Erna's masterful artistry is in every nook and cranny. She is a woman who

pays enormous attention to detail and absolutely nothing escapes her notice. Her philosophy is simple: I only want the best.

From here I was introduced to Angelica, the cook, who was at the time, creating a masterpiece of delicate aromas which wafted throughout the room for some fortunate guests awaiting breakfast. Daniel escorted me back to the salon where I awaited Erna's arrival. I was given the most delicious cup of tea I had ever sipped. I asked what it was. "Our own brew," he replied. There were elderberries floating in the cup, blending aromas which were simply wonderful.

By this time, Erna appeared, a small, delicate and exquisitely dressed woman. She showed me her new addition, the spa, just recently completed and designed in an art deco motif. The spa offers massages, body treatments, facials, manicures and European Kurs: Thalasotherapy (Marine therapy) Krauter (herbal baths). Each treatment room was tiled, bathed in subdued light, and exquisitely furnished. There is even a "couples" treatment room.

Outside the spa, we walked past the Villa below, a two-bedroom, private, gold-studded hideaway which was designed by Erna because film star, Barbra Streisand voiced her need for additional privacy when she visited. It rents for $2950 a day which includes 24-hour butler service.

What Erna has created in the Chateau, Executive Chef Karsten Hart creates for your palate. His philosophy is clearly stated: "We are so fortunate to get our produce fresh daily directly from the Central Valley Farmland—nothing is more exciting than bringing out flavors, textures and colors of an inherently healthy and local product." Under his inspired direction, Erna's Elderberry House kitchen maintains its AAA, Five-Diamond award. The celebrated *Condé Nast Travelers* magazine reader's poll gave his kitchen a perfect score of 100 in 2001.

If all of this were not enough, Erna offers customized tours to Yosemite National Park, just minutes away. One can enjoy a guided tour by Jeep or Hummer, rock climbing, river rafting, hiking, and mountain biking with guides, of course.

My visit over, I reluctantly walked to my car and briefly looked back longingly at the Chateau. I felt as if I had experienced a few enchanted hours at a true fairy tale magic kingdom. Imagine —all of this in our own backyard!

For more information call the Chateau du Sureau: (559) 683-6860
Erna's Elderberry House Restaurant, call: (559) 683-6800
E-mail: chateau@chateausureau.com
Web pages: www.chateausureau.com; www.elderberryhouse.com
Located at: 48688 Victoria Lane in Oakhurst, Calif.

How to get to there:

The estate is about 200 miles from San Francisco. From Fresno or Madera on Highway 99, go northeast on Highway 140 to Highway 49 which ends at Oakhurst. Turn right on Highway 41 and the Chateau is within sight.

Recipes: Erna's Elderberry House Restaurant
From Chef Karsten Hart

Carrot Top Soup With Roasted Carrots
(Serves four)

To prepare the Potato Base:

2 Tbsp. Ground Bacon
1 Tbsp. Olive Oil
1/2 cup Leeks, washed and sliced
1/3 cup Parsnips, peeled and sliced
1/3 cup Celery Root, peeled and sliced
2 Bay Leaves
8 Sprigs fresh Thyme
10 Black Peppercorns
4 Cups Chicken Stock
1 small Russet Potato (about 1/2 cup), peeled and chopped.

Instructions:

Render (separate) fat from bacon in a heavy pot over medium heat. Add olive oil, leeks, parsnips and celery root. Sauté vegetables until they begin to soften. Prepare a sachet by tying bay leaves, thyme and peppercorns in a cheesecloth pouch. Add sachet, stock and potatoes to the pot and cook until potatoes are done. Transfer to a blender and purée until smooth.

To add the Carrot Tops and complete the Soup:

2 Bunches Carrot Tops, washed and chopped
1/4 cup Heavy Cream
1 Tbsp. Unsalted Butter
Salt and freshly ground White Pepper

In a separate pot of boiling water, blanch the chopped carrot tops. Strain and add to the blender. Purée completely into potato base. Remove from blender and strain back into a soup pot and place over low heat.

Whisk in heavy cream and butter. Adjust seasoning and serve at once, hot, with a garnish of roasted carrots.

Banana Gugelhupf (cake)

(Serves 8)

Ingredients:

1 Stick Unsalted Butter, room temperature
1 cup Granulated Sugar
4 Large Eggs, room temperature
2 cups All Purpose Flour
2 tsp. Baking Powder
Pinch of Salt
2 pinches Cinnamon
1 pinch Nutmeg
1 cup mashed ripe Banana
3/4 cup Light Brown Sugar
1/3 cup Heavy Cream
1 1/2 tsp. Vanilla Extract
Grated Zest of 1 Lemon (about 1 Tbsp.)

Instructions:

Preheat oven to 350 degrees Fahrenheit. Using the paddle attachment, cream butter and sugar together in an electric mixer. Beat until light and fluffy. Add eggs one at a time, fully incorporating before adding the next egg. Sift dry ingredients together and set aside. Whisk bananas, brown sugar, cream and vanilla together. Add half of the dry ingredients to butter, sugar and egg mixture, followed by half of banana mixture. Repeat with remaining halves. Spray Gugelhupf mold (or Bundt Cake pan) with food release and pour mixture into mold. Bake for 50-60 minutes or until a cake tester comes out clean. Remove from mold and allow to cool.

Bouillabaisse de la Maison

Serves 4

Bouillabaisse Ingredients:

2 Tbsp. Olive Oil
1 Small Onion, sliced thinly
1 Bulb Fennel, sliced thinly
1 Medium Carrot, peeled and sliced thinly
1 Bulb Roasted Garlic, with meat removed and puréed
1 cup dry Vermouth
5-6 cups Fish or Chicken Broth
1/2 tsp. Toasted Coriander Seeds, lightly crushed
1/2 tsp. Fennel Seeds, lightly crushed
1 Pinch Saffron
2 Bay Leaves
1 Sprig Thyme, chopped
Small amount Orange Zest
1/4 Bunch Parsley, chopped
2 Medium Tomatoes, peeled, seeded and diced
1 Large Russet Potato, peeled, cut in small cubes and blanched
8 Stems of Basil, Chiffonade,* reserve 6 nice leaves for decoration
2 Tbsp. Pernod
1/2 lb. Fresh Tuna, cut into logs
11 Littleneck Clams
Salt and Pepper to taste

> *Chiffonade cut into thin, fine ribbons

Instructions:

In a large heavy pot, sauté onions, fennel and carrot until soft. Add roasted garlic and Vermouth, reduce until alcohol is cooked off. Add broth, coriander, fennel, orange zest, parsley, thyme, bay leaf and saffron. Simmer until flavors are infused. Add Pernod. Add tomatoes, potatoes, basil, clams and season. Season and sear tuna logs in a heavy pan. Keep rare and reserve. Serve in warmed bowls with grilled French bread. Slice tuna and arrange on top. Decorate with a fresh basil sprig.

Fun facts about Bouillabaisse:

Bouillabaisse originated hundreds of years ago on the coast of Southern France. The beginnings were humble—not much more than cauldron full of the unsold remnants from the day's catch, flavored with local vegetables and spices. Bouillabaisse is now serious business. In recent years, the restaurateurs of Marseille, France developed a charter describing what one must find in the dish for it actually to be called Bouillabaisse.

About Executive Chef Karsten Hart

Originally from Baton Rouge, Louisiana Chef Karsten Hart's influence of the South is apparent in his personal cuisine but the effect of two years spent in Germany and Sicily are exemplified by his culinary diversity. Upon his return to the US he attended Louisiana State University. As many college students do, Chef Karsten worked in various restaurants to support his schooling. In between studies of Psychology and Anthropology he always looked for opportunities to nourish his love for cooking. Chef Karsten's next move was to the culinary Mecca of San Francisco where he attended and graduated from California Culinary Academy.

After completing the CCA Chef Karsten returned to Louisiana to work at the Windsor Court Hotel becoming Sous Chef under Exec. Chef James Overbaugh (previously of Erna's Elderberry House). During Chef Karsten's tenure he and Chef James worked together extensively and also became close friends. In 2003 Chef James returned to The Estate by the Elderberries. Shortly thereafter Chef Karsten joined the Elderberry culinary team and the two chefs once again found themselves cooking side by side. Chef Karsten's talent and passion moved him quickly ahead. During 2004 he went from Sous Chef to Chef de Cuisine and after Chef James became Director of Operations in 2006, Chef Karsten took over the responsibilities of The Estate's Executive Chef. Since then Chef Karsten is at the helm much to the delight of guests and owners. As the person who is now guiding the Estate's culinary direction, he proudly carries forth Erna's long tradition of gastronomic excellence.

Chef Karsten has been featured on the local network television affiliates and on The Travel Channel. His recipes are regularly shared with cooking aficionados during his classes at the Estate.

Many of the rooms on the Wawona Hotel open onto the expansive veranda

Photo by Jay Solmonson

Your Wawona is like a bright green emerald
Set between the sparkling diamonds of Yosemite
Valley's waterfalls and the red riches of the Sequoia[1]

[1]Shirley Sargent, *Yosemite's Historic Wawona*, Flying Spur Press, Yosemite, CA

Photo by Chris Falkenstein

The Wawona Hotel 1876
YOSEMITE NATIONAL PARK

*T*he Wawona Hotel is an imposing and heart-pounding sight at first glance. It belongs in the same category as Tara or Fair Oaks from the movie *Gone With The Wind*. Encircled by huge Sequoias, the entrance to the hotel is what tourists from all over the world describe as spectacular. It has been the grand dame of Yosemite National Park since 1876.

In the early years following statehood, California began to take on the reputation of having magical attributes, especially concerning people's health. As the accolades about the wonder cures of the Valley began to take on the quality of the miraculous, visitors to Yosemite arrived in even greater numbers.

One of these stories derived from an early adventurer into Yosemite Valley—Galen Clark, a forty-three year old New Englander who had such severe health problems that his physician told him his days were numbered. Galen chose to spend them in Yosemite's beautiful meadows and forests. He filed a claim in 1856 on 160 acres, built a log cabin, and roamed bareheaded and barefoot for the next fifty-four years, dying finally at the ripe old age of ninety-six. So much for doctor's advice!

His home marked the beginning of Clark's Station, the predecessor of the Wawona Hotel. On one of these excursions a discussion ensued over the name to call the area abounding in such majestic wonders of the West. Someone mentioned the name Mariposa Grove, another noted that the Nuchu Indians called the big trees *Wah-wo-nahs*. The name stuck.

During these early years, just a handful of people visited Clark's Station. Many of them were preservationists at heart. They wanted to make sure that Wawona's beauty would be kept intact. Senator John Conness of California proposed the creation of the Yosemite Grant and a short time later, President Lincoln signed the bill, consigning Yosemite Valley and the Mariposa grove of Sequoia trees to the State of California in a public trust. Galen Clark was appointed its guardian.

By 1866 there was an inn, a crude bridge, a log cabin and state roads leading into Yosemite, which needed constant repair. With the completion of the Central Pacific Railroad, a line was built in the San Joaquin Valley. From there, tourists could take stagecoaches into the magic wonderland which resulted in many more excited people visiting Yosemite. In 1870 Clark's Station enjoyed an increasing number of visitors, but good roads were still lacking.

In spite of the fact that there were, by this time, three pioneer hotels, access into Yosemite Valley was hazardous and it took a hearty visitor to endure the hours of rough riding over dangerous twists and turns in the road.

In 1876 a large, commodious hotel was built at Big Tree

Station, and in 1882, Big Tree Station's name was changed to Wawona. A legend had begun. President Ulysses S. Grant undertook an around-the-world tour which ended in Yosemite. Other presidents followed: Rutherford B. Hayes arrived in 1880, Teddy Roosevelt in 1902 and the list continues.

In 1884 more buildings were added to the hotel and celebrities followed. Lily Langtry (Lillie Langtry), reputed to be one of the most beautiful women in the world, visited, as did Diamond Jim Brady, William Jennings Bryan and many more. World-class landscape painters arrived, such as Thomas Moran, Thomas Hill and Albert Bierstadt. They added to Yosemite's reputation and its fame spread internationally.

From the beginning Wawona's dining facilities and gourmet food were outstanding. Its gardens supplied fresh vegetables; meat from the area's forest abounded as did fish from the many streams.

With the help of noted naturalist and preservationist John Muir, Yosemite National Park was created in 1890. More people arrived and more hotels were built and as many as eight to eleven passenger stages made their way to America's newest national park.[2]

By 1902 over 8,000 tourists had visited Yosemite. This meant that the Wawona Hotel needed more space. A two-story cottage was built in back of the main hotel. Then came automobiles. This was a kind of salvation, since the time spent traveling on the old stage was reduced by hours.

In 1918 a new annex was added to the hotel, plus a swimming tank, a golf course, an entry fountain, and a spacious new dining room.

Up until 1934, the Wawona had been owned and operated by the Washburn family. After that date, the hotel underwent many changes and several owners. It was eventually purchased by the Curry Company.

Today, the Wawona Hotel has 104 guest rooms, some of

---

[2]Yellowstone National Park was the first national park, created March 1, 1872.

which are open to the large veranda which stretches around the entire front of the hotel. The rooms are housed in six buildings and are furnished with beautiful antiques. Fifty rooms have private baths, the rest share a bath house located nearby.

One of the individuals who makes Wawona unique is Tom Bopp. Beginning in 1983, he signed on as a nightly performer in Wawona's piano parlor. His music includes an historic talk and slide presentation, which he has added for guest's entertainment. This unique combination has made him a regular at the hotel.

For more information call the Wawona Hotel front desk:

(209) 375-6556

Room Reservations: (559) 252-4848 or (559) 253-5635

Dining Room: (209) 375-1425

Fax: (209) 375-1336

Web page: www.YosemitePark.com

How to get to there:

The Wawona Hotel is at the southernmost end of Yosemite National Park. The quickest way is from Highway 49 at Oakhurst, go north on Highway 41 to the hotel. There are also Yosemite entrances from Mariposa on Highway 140 and from Groveland on Highway 120.

Recipes: Wawona Hotel
From Chef Robert Stritzinger

Note: Wild Turkeys have always been native to the Wawona area and have made many appearances on the menus over the years. They can still be found in the surrounding woods or out on the golf course. This is an updated, lightened version by Chef Robert Stritzinger of an old Wawona favorite. And, this recipe was a winner in the Mariposa Chili Cook off.

Wawona White Turkey Chili
(Serves 8)

Ingredients:

> 2 1/2 pounds Turkey Breast meat, diced
> 2 Large Onions, diced
> 2 to 3 Jalapeños, seeded and minced
> 5 Garlic Cloves, minced
> 1 1/2 tsp. Toasted Ground Cumin
> 1 tsp. New Mexico Chile Powder
> 1/2 tsp. Ground Coriander
> 1/2 tsp. Ground White Pepper
> Roux made with 1 cup butter and 1 cup flour, cooled
> 2 quarts Turkey Broth (or substitute chicken broth)
> 4 14 oz. cans White Hominy
> 1 Tbsp. Tabasco® brand Chipotle Sauce
> 5 Poblano Chiles roasted, peeled, seeded, and diced
> 1 pound Fresh Tomatillos, diced
> 12 oz. Fresh Tomatoes, diced
> 3/4 tsp. Salt or to taste
> Shredded Cheese, Lime wedges and Flour Tortillas

Method:

Sauté onions in 1 Tbsp. vegetable oil. Add turkey and sauté until brown. Add garlic and Jalapeños and cook 5 more minutes. Add cumin, New Mexico Chile powder, coriander and white pepper stirring to mix all in. Add the roux and cook to heat through. Add half the stock and bring to a boil stirring constantly. Add the rest of the stock, the hominy, the Tabasco® chipotle sauce, the tomatillos and the tomatoes and simmer 20 minutes— until thickened slightly.

Serve with shredded cheese, fresh cilantro, lime wedges and diced red onion as garnish and hot flour tortillas on the side.

Venison Sausage

Chef Robert found some old Wawona Hotel breakfast menus that featured "Deer Foot Sausage," but could not find a recipe or anyone who knew what it was. Here is a recipe he devised for Venison Breakfast Sausage.

Ingredients:

    4 lbs. ground Venison
    1 lb. Ground Pork
    6 Tbsp. Fresh Sage, minced (or 2 Tbls. Dry)
    2 Tbsp. Garlic, minced
    1 Tbsp. Kosher Salt
    2 tsp. freshly ground Black Pepper
    1 Tbsp. Fresh Ginger, grated
    2 tsp. Red Pepper Flakes

Method:

Mix all ingredients together, form into small patties and cook in a cast iron pan.

Pan-Fried Cornmeal Breaded Trout with Arugula Sauce and Corn Cakes

Ingredients:

    8, 8 oz. Trout with heads off
    Cornmeal
    4 oz. Arugula Pesto Sauce — *(See next page)*
    Fresh Cucumbers and Tomatoes, diced
    1 Recipe Corn Cakes — *(See next page)*
    Simple French or Champagne Vinaigrette

Method:

Wash the trout and pat them dry. Sprinkle them with salt and pepper and dredge in the cornmeal. Fry in a medium hot pan about 2 minutes on each side until lightly browned and cooked through. In the meantime, in another pan, cook the corn cakes flipping them like pancakes when they are browned. Toss the cucumbers and tomatoes with some of the vinaigrette and some of the fresh Arugula. Plate the trout, cucumber salad, and the corn cakes and spoon some of the Arugula Sauce on the trout and the salad and serve.

Corn Cake Batter — *used in recipe on previous page*

Ingredients:

1 cup Fresh Corn, puréed smooth
1/2 cup Heavy Cream
1/2 cup Buttermilk
1 Large Egg and 1 Egg Yolk
1 Tbsp. Vegetable Oil
1 cup Corn Meal
1/2 cup Flour
1 1/2 tsp. Sugar
3/4 tsp.Salt
1/2 tsp. Baking Powder
1/2 tsp. Baking Soda
2 Green Onions, minced
1/2 Small Red Bell Pepper, diced
1/2 cup Fresh Corn Kernals

Method:

Purée the heavy cream and 1 cup corn in the blender 'til smooth then add the buttermilk, eggs and oil to just combine. Mix all the dry ingredients in a mixing bowl and fold in the egg mixture, green onions and rest of corn until just mixed. Fry like pancakes.

Arugula Sauce (used in recipe on previous page)

Ingredients:

2 cups fresh Arugula
3/4 cup Olive Oil
4 Garlic Cloves
1 tsp. Salt
1 tsp. Lemon Juice

Method:

Purée all ingredients in a blender until smooth.

Corn and Potato Hash
Serves 4

Ingredients:
> 2 Russet Potatoes, peeled and diced
> 1 Small Red Bell Pepper, diced
> 2 Poblano Chiles,* peeled, seeded, diced
> 1/2 Medium Onion, diced
> 1 cup Corn
> 1 tsp. Fresh Oregano, minced (or substitute: Chives, Cilantro or Sage)
> 2 Tbsp. Olive Oil

Method:

This recipe is nice when all the vegetables are diced about the size of a corn kernel. Blanch potatoes in boiling water about 7 minutes until just cooked through. Sauté onions and bell peppers 5 minutes then add corn and sauté 3 minutes more. Remove from heat and add poblano chiles and potatoes and mix well. Recipe can be prepared to this point up to 2 days ahead. Heat olive oil in a ten-inch sauté pan until hot, but not smoking. Add hash and sauté until potatoes are lightly browned.

BBQ Salmon with Avocado Aioli
Serves 4

Ingredients:
> Four 6 oz. Salmon Filets

Avocado Aioli:

> 2 Ripe Avocados, mashed
> 1 Tbsp. Lime Juice
> 1 Small Poblano Chile, roasted, peeled, seeded*
> 2 Tbsp. Fresh Cilantro, minced
> 3 Tbsp. Mayonnaise
> 1/2 tsp. Salt, or to taste

Method:

Purée the Avocado Aioli ingredients in a food processor until smooth.

20

BBQ Salmon Rub

Ingredients:

Four 6 oz. Salmon Filets
3/4 cup New Mexico Chile Powder**
1/4 cup Paprika
1 Tbsp. Ground White Pepper
1 Tbsp. Mexican Oregano, toasted
1 Tbsp. Whole Coriander, toasted and ground
2 Tbsp. Cumin, toasted and ground
1 Tbsp. Kosher Salt
1 Tbsp. Sugar
1 tsp. Cayenne Chile

Final serving procedure:

Rub the salmon steaks with the BBQ rub mix and grill on low heat until cooked through. Top with the Avocado Aioli (previous page).

***Poblano Chiles** are fairly common in most supermarket produce sections. They are dark green and kind of heart-shaped. Sometimes they are called **Pasillas**. It is easy to roast them over an open flame on your gas stove until they are charred all over. Then put them in a plastic bag for 10 minutes to steam, then peel them in a bowl of water.

Do NOT use commercial chili powder as it has other ingredients already mixed in. **New Mexico Chile Powder is pure ground chiles with nothing else added. It may be hard to find, but it turns up pretty regularly with Mexican spices in supermarkets that cater to a Mexican community or try a Mexican specialty store, if you have one in your community.

Chef Robert Stritzinger

Chef Robert Stritzinger is a certified Chef de Cuisine at the Wawona since December 2004. He has won many cooking awards, including two A.C.F. (American Culinary Federation) Gold Medals and several Chili Cook-offs.

The Ahwahnee Hotel — Illustration by Christine Holman

The Ahwahnee under construction — 1927

Photo courtesy of DNC Parks & Resorts

The Ahwahnee Hotel 1927
YOSEMITE NATIONAL PARK

*T*here are larger, more spacious hotels in California, but there is nothing that compares to the implausibly breathtaking setting and character of The Ahwahnee Hotel. Architectural historians refer to this as the "power of place." Nestled among Yosemite Falls, Glacier Point, Half Dome and the Royal Arches, The Ahwahnee rises from the floor of a world seemingly forgotten by time.

For thousands of years Yosemite Valley's existence was known to only a few Miwok (Ahwahnechee) Indians. For them, the Valley was known as "Ahwahnee, the place of a gaping mouth."

The Ahwahnee's isolation, unfortunately, would not last. Nothing could stop waves of eager miners searching for the ever elusive promise of wealth initiated by the Gold Rush. Persistent gold seekers pressed ever further into the pristine world of the Yosemite

23

Valley. The seclusion of the rugged Sierras had protected the tribes, but in 1851 their ideal life came to an end when an armed military battalion was sent into the valley to remove the Indians from their ancestral homes by force. One member of that military group was so moved by the beauty of the place, he named it Yosemite, thinking that this was the name the Indians called it themselves. Actually, the word was a corruption of the word *o-ham-i-te*, meaning grizzly bear.

Other intruders followed. They built cabins, homesteaded, and in 1857, the first formal campground was begun. That same year the Sentinel Hotel was built. It was hardly luxurious. The rooms were drafty and there was a communal bath. It helped serve Yosemite's visitors until 1925. Other hotels and lodges followed, but none were year around and few could be described as truly commodious. In spite of narrow, often impassable roads, the beauty of the valley rewarded early visitors with unforgettable vistas well worth the difficult trek. Yosemite's fame spread.

By 1915 stagecoaches and buggies were increasingly replaced with the horseless carriages as the age of the automobile arrived. Roads were subsequently improved and tourism to the area began in earnest after the 1920s. As the park's reputation grew, so too did the demands for a year-around hotel.

Before The Ahwahnee could be built, however, the national park system (created in 1916) needed a visionary individual to bring the dream of a first-class hotel to fruition. Stephen Mather stepped into that role. Chosen to head the park service, he was well aware that Yellowstone National Park, the Grand Canyon National Park and Glacier National Park had magnificent hotels, but not Yosemite. He felt that better facilities were necessary to meet the needs of a growing number of sophisticated visitors now arriving from all over the world. One of those famous visitors was Lady Astor, England's first female member of Parliament. The best Yosemite could offer her at the time was the Sentinel Hotel. It was not up to her elite upper-class European traveler's requirements. When Mr. Mather heard of her indignation, he provided the much-needed inspiration to see that plans for a truly memorable hotel were begun. The hotel would not only provide year-around access, but would also cater to the world's wealthiest clientele.

The task of designing such a hotel fell to Gilbert S. Underwood, a southern California architect. Mr. Underwood was asked to design a fireproof structure which would accommodate 100 guests. His goal was to give the hotel the look of a large commodious home. Most important, the edifice should be in keeping with its ancient landscape. His designs for an exterior of concrete

The Ahwahnee Hotel under construction — 1927

Photo courtesy of DNC Parks & Resorts

made to look like rough-hewn timber, would meet the demands of the central Sierra Nevada's harsh winters, but its features would merge with the Indian lore, the tall pines, and the massive granite cliffs that rose above it.

The first time I visited Yosemite, I was about nine years old. My father had described the park to me in great detail from his previous trips made in the 1920s when he purchased his first car. In those days, getting to Yosemite over Tioga's narrow precipitous road was quite an adventure, not undertaken by the timid motorist. For a southern Californian who had never seen snow, except from a distance, my father's vivid descriptions of a kind of winter wonderland had taken on the attributes of a magical kingdom. The long, weary trip north only added to my expectations. Each serpentine bend in the road heightened my anticipation. When, at last, the broad valley came into view, like children everywhere, I scampered toward Mirror Lake and the dozens of deer meandering peacefully around its edge. I had never seen a "wild" animal before and the idea of actually feeding them was simply unimaginable. The spectacular fire fall from Glacier Point that evening ranked a close second to that first indelible experience. Even now, when I arrive at the entrance to Yosemite Valley, all those early memories come flooding back.

As if to purposely heighten the expectation of The Ahwahnee's first-time guests, famous landscape designer Frederick Law Olmsted, created an imposing stone gate near the entrance to the hotel, elevating the suspense of arrival. The anticipation is further prolonged as one enters the hotel lobby. One's first impression is dramatic and unforgettable. But the grand finale is yet to come. The great lounge lies ahead, expanding in all directions, extending up to a massive overhead, beamed ceiling. It is one of the most striking sensual perceptions that visitors remember. Seeing the entry and lounge for the first time is like passing through layers of Native American History displayed in a museum-like atmosphere. The wonder is that The Ahwahnee still maintains its original authentic decor. At the time it was built, the likely choices for its interior design could have been bearskin rugs and buffalo horns. Instead, the most professional team of experts were consulted to render their enormous talents—covering the choice of fabrics, rugs, paint, custom-made, wrought iron lighting fixtures, mosaics and a wide variety of furniture, crafted with an unwavering appreciation of the finest workmanship in the world. The fact that the designers chose to profile Yosemite's indigenous people, elevating and highlighting the appreciation of their artwork, was unusual for the time. Indian baskets from the Yurok, Hoopa and Pomo tribes still adorn the beautiful lobby.[1]

The Ahwahnee's Lounge

Photo John Bellenis Photography

The menu at The Ahwahnee offers all the superb dishes guests have come to expect at an elegant hotel. There is the traditional Salmon, poached in white wine; Long Island Duckling; Lamb roasted in herbs and garlic; and Prime Rib served with Yorkshire Pudding. These dishes are further enhanced by the enormous

---

[1]Note: none of these are the original Yosemite tribes. Different spellings of many of these Indian tribes vary as per the source.

Photo John Bellenis Photography

The Ahwahnee's Dining Room

variety of international fare which the hotel chefs present with all their succulent, exotic aromas.

But it is Christmas that is most memorable at The Ahwahnee. The most spectacular culinary gala in all of California is staged each year as winter descends upon the park. At dusk on Christmas Eve, a huge Yule Log is lit. Ballads sung by a druid princess are followed by the arrival of Saint Nick.

The following evening the Bracebridge Dinner begins. Based on a tale about Christmas Day at Bracebridge Hall in Yorkshire, England in the seventeenth century, this grand festival has been held since 1927. Over 350 fortunate guests are treated to a "Christmas that never was, but a Christmas that lives in everyone's hearts."[2] For three hours, the dining room's 130-foot long hall with 34-foot high ceiling becomes an English Renaissance extravaganza. Gongs

---

[2]Keith S. Walklet, *The Ahwahnee: Yosemite's Grand Hotel*, DNC Parks and Resorts at Yosemite, 2004

chime, lights dim and a colorful entourage of costumed choristers enter the huge room singing. The feast that follows is fit for royalty. Elaborately adorned tables with an accompaniment of singing minstrels enchant the guests with their songs. Courses (which vary yearly) may consist of Maine Lobster or a poached fish with sauce and marbled potatoes, poultry with a spicy dressing, and huge platters of boar's heads are presented by a squire who announces the feast with great fanfare. "Another dish of ancient name deserves high rank with gesture brief, I knight thee—Sir Loin, Baron of Beef." All of this is washed down with ample quantities of liquid refreshments, followed by a creamy Plum Pudding and Wassail Punch which brings the evening's festivities to an end.

Kings, queens, sheik's, emperors and four American presidents have stayed at The Ahwahnee Hotel. When President John F. Kennedy visited in 1963, he flew into the valley by helicopter and is the only American President to stay at the hotel while still in office. In 1983 Her Majesty Queen Elizabeth II and Prince Philip of Great Britain arrived. Due to security concerns, all reservations for rooms during the royal stay were rescheduled.

Hundreds of movie and stage legends have also stayed at the hotel. In 1947 Judy Garland entertained Desi Arnaz and Lucille Ball late at night around one of the two Steinways in the lobby. Many film stars have spent their honeymoon here and countless films have been shot beneath Bridal Veil Falls, Half Dome and the velvet green expanse of lawns surrounding The Ahwahnee.

Today The Ahwahnee Hotel remains as timeless, pristine and luxurious as it did when I first saw it as a young and impressionable girl. Artists continue to paint its beauty, photographers continue to capture its vistas, but nothing is ever quite like that first extraordinary vision of the massive Royal Arches under which The Ahwahnee Hotel resides. Here, the tradition of superb hospitality and gourmet dining continues.

For more information, call The Ahwahnee: (209) 372-1399
Room Reservations: (559) 252-4848
Fax: (209) 372-1453
Web page: www.yosemitepark.com

How to get to The Ahwahnee Hotel:

There are four Yosemite National Park entrances:

- *East Entrance:* From Highway 395, take Highway 120 over Tioga Pass into the park. At Crane Flat turn left to Yosemite Valley.

- *West Entrance:* From Highway 120, take Highway 49 toward Moccasin. Take 120 east through Groveland into the park.

- *Southwest Entrance:* From Merced take Highway 140 into the park

- *South Entrance:* From Fresno take Highway 41 into the park.

The Ahwahnee Chef Percy S. Whatley

Chef Percy S. Whatley is the Executive Chef of The Ahwahnee, Yosemite National Park's four-diamond, historic national landmark hotel. Mr. Whatley was named to his position in November 2005 and oversees all aspects of food production at the hotel.

He began his career at the Pizza Deck in Curry Village. Later he departed briefly, earning an A.S. Degree in Business Management from The College of the Redwoods in Eureka, California. He then returned to Yosemite, assuming the summer management of White Wolf Lodge in the High Sierra region of the park. Mr. Whatley then joined the ranks of The Ahwahnee, holding multiple kitchen positions including Lead Line Cook.

In 1996 Mr. Whatley enrolled at the prestigious Culinary Institute of America (CIA) in Hyde Park, New York. He then worked at the Hyatt Regency Resort in South Carolina and graduated from the CIA with honors in 1997.

In the summer of 1999, Mr. Whatley became the Executive Chef at the Wawona Hotel. He earned the distinguished Certified Chef de Cuisine title in April 2002 through the American Culinary Federation. He assumed responsibility for all aspects of food production at the Wawona including weddings, banquets and lawn barbecues.

Mr. Whatley returned to The Ahwahnee in the fall of 2003. He soon accepted the position of Executive Sous Chef and began the use of organic and sustainable ingredients which allowed him to be a major contributor to DNC Parks & Resorts' environmental initiatives.

Chef Whatley has graciously included the 2005 menu for the famous Christmas Bracebridge Dinner!

Recipes: The Ahwahnee Hotel
From Executive Chef Percy S. Whatley

Bracebridge Dinner 2005

Peking Duck Leg Confit
with Roasted Butternut Squash Risotto
and Preserved Kumquat Cranberry Relish
(Serves 8)

Ingredients:
>   8 each Duck Legs, whole quarter (including thighs)
>   2 Tbsp. Kosher Salt
>   2 Tbsp. Brown Sugar
>   3 each Star Anise
>   2 each Cinnamon Sticks
>   6 each Whole Clove
>   4 each Whole Allspice
>   2 tsp. Orange Zest
>   1 tsp. Lemon Zest
>   1 tsp. Black Peppercorns
>   4 each Whole Fresh Thyme Leaves
>   1 quart, Rendered Duck Fat, as needed

Instructions:

1. Combine all spices, sugar, zests, and salt, mix with hands to incorporate. Rub all areas of the duck legs. Set them in a flat, glass baking dish, cover with plastic wrap, and cure them in the refrigerator overnight.

2. Remove from marinade and discard spices.

3. Preheat oven to 275° F.
Heat a large skillet or braising pan over medium heat. Add 2 Tbsp. of duck fat to the pan and brown both sides of each leg—a few at a time. When complete, add all legs to the pan and add the remaining duck fat, enough to cover the legs completely. Cook, covered, in the oven for 6 hours. Removed legs from fat and let drain. Reserve for the dinner. *If cooking this the day before the dinner, refrigerate overnight and heat again in the rendered fat.*

4. Cool fat and strain through a strainer or an oil filter, save in the refrigerator for up to a month or in the freezer indefinitely.

Preserved Kumquat Cranberry Relish
Yield: 1 Cup (8 - 1 oz. portions)

Ingredients:

1/2 cup Kumquats, cut in half
1/2 cup Cranberries, frozen, whole
1 tsp. Small Yellow Onion, diced
1/2 tsp. Fresh Ginger, peeled and minced
1/4 tsp. Serrano Chili, seeds removed, minced
1 tsp. Fresh Cilantro, chopped
1/2 cup Water
2 Tbsp. Red Wine Vinegar
2 Tbsp. Honey
1 tsp. Sugar, Granulated
1/2 each Cinnamon Stick

Method:

Combine all ingredients into a small sauce pan and cook over low heat until almost all the moisture is evaporated. The consistency should be much like a typical cranberry sauce (jelly) purchased in the supermarket.

Bring relish to room temperature and serve over the Duck Legs. *This preparation can be kept in the refrigerator for up to 3 weeks.*

Roasted Butternut Squash Risotto

Yield: 8 portions

Ingredients:

1/2 lb. Arborio or Carnoroli Rice
1/2 cup Small Yellow Onion, diced
1 cup Butternut Squash, roasted, skin removed, pulp only
1 qt. + 1 cup Chicken Stock, hot, as needed
1 Tbsp. Whole Butter
3 Tbsp. Parmesan Cheese, grated
1 tsp. Fresh Oregano, chopped
Kosher Salt, as needed to taste
White Pepper, as needed to taste

Method:

1. Cook onions in butter until translucent, add rice and continuously stir with a wooden spoon to coat rice with butter.

2. Add 1/2 of the chicken stock, and the squash, stirring constantly. As the rice continues to simmer it is very important you do not stop stirring to prevent lumping and scorching.

3. Add more stock as the rice becomes thick and creamy, adding more every time the rice becomes too thick. As the opaque color of the rice starts to turn more of a translucent color, you are getting very close to the rice being done. Taste and make sure the rice is not crunchy, if so, add a little more stock and continue to stir.

4. When the rice is cooked to your liking, fold in parmesan cheese and oregano. Season with salt and white pepper to taste. Serve immediately.

Ginger Poached Sacramento Sturgeon
with Sticky Rice Cake, Lemon Grass-Chili Emulsion

Yield: 6 portions

Ingredients:

1 lb. Sturgeon Filet, skin off, cut into 6 portions

Sticky Rice Cake

Ingredients:

1 cup Calrose Rice
1 cup Water
1 cup Fresh Orange Juice
2 Tbsp. Scallions, sliced thin
2 tsp. small Red Bell Pepper, diced
2 tsp. small Green Bell Pepper, diced
1 tsp. Black Sesame Seeds, use white if not available
1 tsp. Canola Oil
1/2 tsp. Kosher or Sea Salt

1. Steam rice in water, salt and orange juice for 30 minutes. If there is no way to steam it, place liquid, salt and rice in an appropriate size sauce pan and cook over low heat, or use a rice cooker. When completely cooked remove from heat and let rest for 10 minutes before fluffing with a fork.

2. Sauté bell pepper in oil over medium heat until slightly limp. Reserve.

3. Combine all ingredients and let cool slightly, enough to handle.

4. Mold in a cookie cutter or a loaf pan. If using a loaf pan, spray with pan release and press firmly to stick the rice grains together. Let cool to room temperature and turn the rice out of the pan. Slice a 1/4 to 1/2 inch thick.

5. For service, pan fry cakes in a little Canola oil over medium low heat until lightly browned.

Poaching Liquid for Sturgeon:

Ingredients:

    3 stalks Lemon Grass, roughly chopped
    6 oz. Fresh Ginger, unpeeled, roughly chopped
    1 tsp. Dried Chili Flakes
    1 tsp. Sriracha Sauce, or chili paste
    1/4 cup Lime Juice
    1/4 cup White Wine
    1/4 cup Large Onion, diced
    1/4 cup Celery, large stalk, diced
    3 ea. Garlic Cloves, whole, bruised
    1/4 cup. Kosher or Sea Salt
    1 1/2 qts. Water

1. Combine all ingredients in a sauce or stock pot, boil for 25 minutes.

2. Strain through a fine mesh strainer to remove solids.

3. To poach, have the liquid deep enough to place all portions of the fish. Bring the liquid up to 175° F, or where you can see just a couple of bubbles (not boiling, but almost).

4. Poach fish, completely submerged, for 6 minutes.

Lemon Grass-Chili Emulsion (Dressing)

Ingredients:

    2 hearts Lemon Grass, roughly chopped
    2 cloves Garlic, roughly chopped
    1 tsp. Dried Chili Flakes
    1 cup Coconut Milk
    2 Tbsp. Mayonnaise
    2 tsp. Lime Juice
    1/2 tsp. Salt, Kosher or Sea

Combine all ingredients into a blender. Blend on high for 1 minute until smooth; strain through a fine mesh strainer.
Refrigerate until ready to use. Drizzle directly over the fish.

Sierra Nevada Pale Ale &
Fiscalini Farms® Cheddar Cheese Soup

Serves 8 (8 oz. Portions)

Ingredients:

> 1/2 cup Onion, fined diced
> 1 Tbsp. Garlic, minced
> 6 Slices of Bacon, diced
> 1 Tbsp. Butter
> 1/2 cup All-purpose Flour
> 1 1/2 Quarts Vegetable Broth
> 1-12oz. Bottle Sierra Nevada Pale Ale Beer
> 2 cups Heavy Cream
> 2 Tbsp. Worcestershire Sauce
> 2 tsp. prepared Horseradish
> 2 Tbsp. Dijon Mustard
> 2 Bay Leaves
> Salt, to taste
> Pepper, to taste
> 1/2 lb. Ficalini Farms® Cheddar Cheese, shredded
> Sourdough Croutons, optional

Preparation:

Heat a 6 qt. stockpot over a medium heat and add the diced bacon. Cook until bacon is 2/3s done. Add the butter, onions and garlic and continue cooking an additional 3 minutes or until the onions are translucent. When ready, mix in the flour to make your roux, cook for additional 3 minutes. Using a whisk, slowly add the vegetable stock and heavy cream until it has all been incorporated. Bring contents of stockpot to a boil; add the Worcestershire Sauce, mustard, horseradish and Bay leaves. Reduce heat and simmer for 20 minutes.

Add the Ale and cheddar cheese, whisk soup until smooth and all the cheese has melted and has been thoroughly incorporated. Remove the bay leaves, adjust the seasonings, and keep hot until you are ready to serve. Serve topped with Sourdough Croutons, if desired.

Roasted Granny Smith Apple Bisque
with Apple Ginger Compote & Curry Crème Fraiche

Yield: 8 portions

Ingredients:

1 lb. Granny Smith Apples, peeled, cored, diced
2 Tbsp. Whole Butter
1/2 cup Onions, diced
1/4 cup Celery, diced
1/4 cup Parsnip, diced
1/4 cup Leek, Whites only, diced
1 tsp. Garlic, minced
1 1/2 qts. Vegetable Stock, Clear
1/2 cup White Wine
1/4 cup Apple Cider Vinegar
1/2 cup Heavy Cream
1/4 cup Long Grain White Rice
2 each Cinnamon Stick, Whole
1/4 tsp. Ground Cardamom
1/4 tsp. Ground Coriander
1 tsp. Fresh Thyme, chopped
2 each Bay Leaf
1/2 tsp. White Pepper, to taste
2 tsp. Salt, to taste

Method:

Preheat oven to 350° F.
1. Melt 1 Tbsp. of butter over medium heat in a sauce pot. Place apples in a mixing bowl and pour melted butter over apples, toss to coat with butter. Spread apples evenly over a cookie sheet and roast for 30 minutes or until lightly caramelized. Remove and let cool slightly.
2. In a large stock pot (1 gallon), sweat onions, celery, parsnip, leeks and garlic in remaining butter. Cook until onions are translucent.
3. Add apples and remaining ingredients except rice. Bring to simmer and add rice stirring constantly until simmering again. Stir occasionally simmering soup over medium low heat with a cover for 30 minutes. Remove from heat.
4. Remove cinnamon sticks and bay leaves prior to moving on with next

37

step. In a blender, fill the blending pitcher only half way to prevent any overflow, blend on low, moving to high speed until smooth. Strain through the finest strainer available into a clean sauce pot. Keep repeating this step until all of the soup is blended. If you have an immersion blender (stick blender) this step can be done in the pot it was cooked in, then strained into a clean pot.

5. Replace back on the stove over low heat and cover to keep warm for the meal.

Apple Ginger Compote

Ingredients:

> 1 cup Granny Smith Apples, peeled, cored, diced
> 1 Tbsp.Fresh Ginger, peeled, minced
> 1/4 cup Apple Cider Vinegar
> 1/4 cup Brown Sugar
> 1 Cinnamon Stick, Whole
> pinch Salt
> 1/4 cup Water

Method:

Place all ingredients in a small sauce pot and cook for 30 minutes adding more water as needed to prevent burning. The final consistency should be jam-like and the apples should be soft and palatable.
Cool to room temperature, garnish the center of the soup.

Curried Créme Fraiche

Ingredients:

> 1/2 cup Créme Fraiche (if not available, use sour cream)
> 1 tsp. Curry Powder, Madras
> pinch Salt
> pinch Granulated Sugar

Method:

1. Combine all ingredients, stir to incorporate.
2. Place a dollop over the compote in the center of the soup.

Scallop and Shiitake Mushroom Wellington

Yield: 8 Portions

Ingredients:

16 Scallops, U8 (means large 8/lb.) cleaned, sliced crosswise
16 Shiitake Mushroom Caps, seasoned, roasted
8 Menlo Wrappers, (thin egg roll wrappers), cut in half
Egg Wash, as needed
6 oz. Caramelized Shallots (see recipe below)
Salt, as needed
Black Pepper, as needed
8 oz. Truffle Vinaigrette (recipe next page)
4 tomatoes Plum Tomato Confit (recipe next page)
8 cups loose Spinach Leaves, clean

Scallop Wellington Method (after all items are prepared)

1. Build a Napoleon-style stack with a layer of half scallop, shiitake mushroom, another half scallop then a 1/2 tsp. of the caramelized shallots (recipe below). Season the scallops with salt and black pepper.
2. Wrap this in a half sheet of Menlo wrapper, brush the edges of the wrapper with egg wash to help seal, and loosely closing the sides of the wrapper.
3. Heat a deep fryer to 350° or a skillet deep enough for the packages to float using Canola Oil. Deep fry for 3 minutes or until golden brown.
4. Remove and slice each roll in half exposing the Napoleon inside.
5. Toss the spinach in Truffle Vinaigrette and also use some for around the plate or platter. Garnish with Tomato Confit and place the Wellingtons around the spinach.

Caramelized Shallots

Ingredients:

6 oz. Shallots, sliced.
1/2 stick Whole Butter
2 Tbsp. Sugar

continued

pinch Salt
pinch Black Pepper

Combine into a large sauce pan, slowly caramelize over medium-low heat stirring occasionally until a dark golden brown color is reached. Cool and reserve.

Truffle Vinaigrette

Ingredients:

1/2 oz. Truffles, chopped (fresh or canned).
1/2 oz. Truffle Oil
5 oz. Canola Oil
1 Tbsp. Shallots, diced, sweated in Canola oil until translucent
1 oz. Red Wine, drinkable
1 oz. Red Wine Vinegar
1/4 tsp. Dijon Mustard
pinch Salt
pinch Black Pepper
1 tsp. Fresh Tarragon, chopped

1. Cook red wine and reduce by half.
2. Combine all liquids except oils and add mustard, whisk to incorporate
3. Whisk in oil slowly, season with salt, pepper and tarragon. Reserve in refrigerator up to 3 days.

Plum Tomato Confit

4 Plum Tomatoes quartered, peeled, seeded, (cut into petals)
1/4 cup Extra Virgin Olive Oil
2 Basil Leaves
2 Garlic Cloves, bruised
1 Thyme Sprigs, whole
3 Black Peppercorns, whole

1. Infuse oil with herbs and garlic over medium heat for 15 minutes
2. Pour hot oil over tomatoes and let sit for 20 minutes
3. Cut each petal in half, four pieces per portion.
4. Serve at room temperature.

The Ahwahnee Bracebridge Wassail Punch

Yield: Approximately 1/2 gallon (Ten 6 oz. portions)

Ingredients:

1 qt. Apple Juice
1 qt. Cranberry Juice
5 oz. Port Wine
4 Whole Cloves
1 Star Anise Seed
1 Tbsp. Dried Hibiscus
Dried Orange Rind, from 1/2 orange
1 Whole Cinnamon Stick
1/2 oz. Ginger, Grated

Method:

Place all ingredients into a sauce pot and simmer for 30 minutes. Strain through a fine sieve into a punch bowl. Serve warm in coffee mugs.
Don't forget to sing WASSAIL!

"O Oysters, said the Carpenter,
'You've had a pleasant run!
Shall we be trotting home again?
But answer came there none—
And this was scarcely odd, because

They'd eaten every one."

Alice In Wonderland and
Through the Looking Glass
by Lewis Carroll —1832 -1898

Hotel Jeffery drawing by John Cross

Hotel Jeffery 1851
COULTERVILLE

*T*wenty-five years separated my first visit to Coulterville from the one I made in October 2006 to the Hotel Jeffery. I had passed through the town on numerous occasions, but had not stopped long enough to smell the roses. When I drove through the town recently in search of information on the hotel, it was as if time had stood still for the small hamlet located at the crossroads to Yosemite.

The community was getting ready for a visitation of ghosts and goblins as preparations for Halloween were getting underway. Fall was in the air, leaves were turning orange and red and a wispy breeze felt almost unsettling. I couldn't help but recall the story of Sleepy Hollow—Washington Irving's immortal story about the headless horseman as he goes riding through a

43

mysterious dark countryside. "A drowsy dreamy influence seemed to hang over the land as if the place was bewitched."[1]

The Hotel Jeffery is uniquely situated at the convergence of two major Highways, 49 and 132. Whichever highway you take, you cannot miss the hotel. The three-story architectural and historical gem commands your attention, not the least of which is due to a 100 year-old Wisteria plant which winds its sinuous way over and around wooden columns extending across the entire side and front of the hotel. It is a welcome sight for the weary traveler, the historian, the preservationist and all those men and women who yearn to become time travelers, if only for an afternoon or evening. Here you have the luxury of basking in a world that invites you to partake in one of the most colorful eras in California history.

The hotel boasts of having one of the oldest operating saloons in California, dating back to the 1850s. When I opened the door of the Magnolia Bar, my first sensation was that I had just stepped back in time from the 21st to the 19th century. The inside was large, dark, and cavernous with a bar that almost stretched the entire length of the room. The original wooden plank floors are still pristine, though somewhat uneven. People have, after all, trod these floors over the past century and a half. It does not take much to imagine John Wayne walking through the swinging saloon doors with six shooters in hand ready to settle an old score.

Today, locals, passers-by and guests crowd into the bar on a Friday or Saturday night and things get very lively. A pianist pounds out the musical strains of the Old West and behind the bar is a friendly bartender who sets 'em up, just like they did way back when. Thirty-inch thick rock and adobe walls built by Mexican masons have endured through three fires. If you glance up at the 25-foot ceiling, there are beautiful oil lamps hanging mid-way down the room amid hundreds of one dollar bills which must have taken an awfully tall ladder to put in place. From the saloon you enter the hotel lobby and front desk. It

---

[1] Washington Irving, The Legend of Sleepy Hollow, New York: P.F. Collier & Son, 1917.

wasn't always like that. Originally there were two separate buildings with an alley in between. The older bar and saloon on one side and the hotel with a passageway in between on the other. Owner Cherylann escorted me through the old alleyway, now enclosed, where I could plainly see the thick adobe walls. These are the walls that saved the hotel from succumbing to the fires that destroyed the town three times: in 1859, 1879 and 1899.

As a life-long preservationist what I enjoyed so much about Hotel Jeffery is that it has been restored magnificently, but not at the expense of the flavor and authenticity of its past. Wherever possible, the old has remained intact. When Peter and Cherylann Schimmelfennig purchased the hotel in 2003, they had a lot of work awaiting them. They rolled up their sleeves and worked wonders. Cherylann likes to refer to the result as a living museum.

The town has not changed much in the 154 years since its founding. The sign just outside of town says there are 115 souls who live within the city. How do the owners, Peter and Cheryann, attract the number of guests necessary to keep this beautiful structure financially viable? There simply must be bucket loads of artistic know-how to undertake a project like this, pour in hard-earned dollars and attract people from far and wide to keep the Jeffery clothed in all its century-old charm.

I was awed. Perhaps I tend to become somewhat sentimental when I see work like this and the people that love these old buildings enough to bring them back to life so everyone can enjoy them. We have monuments all over the Mother Lode which the State of California places on streets so that tourists can read about our history. Yet I have often wished that someone would erect monuments to those dedicated people who restore and preserve these gems of our past. Without them our trips along historic highways would not be nearly as interesting.

In Coulterville, you can still peruse the old streets, look at the old buildings in town which haven't changed much from when they were first built—when gold fever drove men by the thousands to find their way to the foothills of the Sierra Nevada.

Across from the hotel is the Northern Mariposa County

History Center, once a large three-story hotel, named appropriately The Coulter Hotel, which fell prey to the 1899 fire that raced through town. There, one can peruse the history of the town, visit the Wells Fargo office and see many of the treasured exhibits which are displayed.

The museum takes you back to 1849 when George Coulter and his wife came to the Mariposa gold fields, having traveled overland in a covered wagon from Pennsylvania. A friend enticed Coulter to take a look at some promising "diggins" along Maxwell Creek. When Coulter arrived, he established a store, nothing more than a blue tent, and hung out a flag. His tent and flag became such a familiar landmark that people called it, Banderita, or "little flag."

Soon other buildings made their appearance and the site was named Coulterville. Rooming houses, saloons and hotels sprang up to take care of the many people who came to find El Dorado ("the gilded one" in Spanish) and, eventually, there were over twenty-five saloons echoing with the sound of music, loose women, drinking, gambling, and a few brawls now and again. Ten hotels stood in Coulterville when the town expanded to accommodate over 10,000 people. The community welcomed nine nationalities, 1,000 of whom were Chinese. The time traveler can stop by the Sun Sun Wo Co. mercantile store, much like it was when the Wo family arrived. Running the local grocery, they served the men and women who came to mine the more than 200 hard rock mines that were established when millions in gold were dug out of the nearby hills.

On my visit I sat down with owner, Cherylann, in the saloon. The hotel, she explained, had thirty rooms originally but now has twenty-one larger rooms, all with hand-made quilts and antiques. Each room will eventually have its own name and history pertinent to that theme.

President Teddy Roosevelt visited in 1902 on his way to Yosemite and returned on more than one occasion. I also learned that the hotel was originally built as a Fandago Hall for stage-coaches on their way to Yosemite. There are sitting rooms on each floor with a television and all the accouterments guests enjoy during their stay. There are five rooms with private baths and there are large communal baths on each floor.

I was escorted to the banquet hall, a huge room which was in the process of being decorated for Halloween. It could easily seat hundreds of people. Great for wedding receptions.

Downstairs I was shown the dining room, patterned after Grandma's parlor. It seats 100, but reminds me of a large dining room in a Victorian home with antique cabinets filled to capacity with treasures that any Grandmother would have collected. Cherylann pointed to an original Mexican bar door, broken in a brawl, but restored and incorporated into the decor of the room. Pictures hang everywhere over the rich, tapestried walls.

And what about ghosts? There are seventeen ghosts in the Hotel Jeffery! Cherylann gave me a whole packet of testimonials from guests telling of their friendly experience with the spirits. All of the hotel's unique inhabitants were tranquil and calm.

When I finished my tour, I returned to the saloon and ordered lunch. I was served a delicious clam chowder soup, piping hot, with freshly baked rolls. If this is any indication of the food at the Jeffery, I wholeheartedly recommend it. An executive chef is in charge of their four-star dining room.

The owners offer a large variety of tourist's packages with trips to Yosemite and Moaning Cavern and lots of excursions to other Gold Rush communities. Come on down and stay awhile.

For more information, call Hotel Jeffery: (209) 878-3471

E-Mail: info@HotelJefferyGold.com

Web page: www.hoteljefferygold.com

Location: No. 1 Main Street, Coulterville, California

Mail: Hotel Jeffery, P.O. Box 150, Coulterville, CA 95311

How to get there:
From Modesto on Highway 99, take Highway 132 heading east to Coulterville on Historic Highway 49.

Recipes: Hotel Jeffery

Appetizer

Crab Cakes with Coconut Banana Sauce

Ingredients:

> 2 lb. Crab meat
> 1/4 cup Red Bell Pepper, finely chopped
> 1/4 cup Yellow Bell Pepper, finely chopped
> 1/4 cup Red Onion, finely chopped
> 1/4 cup Celery, finely chopped
> 1/4 cup Old Bay Seasoning®
> 1/4 cup Lemon Juice
> 1 Tbsp. Coriander
> 1/4 cup Mayonnaise
> 1 tsp. Red Pepper Flakes
> Bread Crumbs for coating

Method:

Sauté bell peppers, red onion and celery. Add remaining ingredients, except bread crumbs, and form into 1 1/2 oz. cakes. Roll in enough bread crumbs to hold the cakes without falling apart.

Coconut Banana Sauce

Ingredients:

> 1 cup Coconut Milk, reduce
> 2 drops of Banana Extract

Cook coconut milk until it thickens. Add banana extract. Serve sauce warm over the crab cakes.

48

The Trading Post Pan-Seared Salmon

Ingredients:

8 oz. Salmon Fillet, skin off, pre-boned
Oil
Butter
Lemon Pepper seasoning
Old Bay Seasoning®
1/4 cup Red or Yellow Bell Peppers, julienne
8 oz. Pineapple Juice
1 Tbsp. Honey
1 Tbsp. Soy Sauce
1 tsp. Ginger (dry powder)
1 tsp. Coriander

Method:

1. Season salmon fillet with lemon pepper and Old Bay Seasoning®
2. Pan-sear and finish in oven
3. Add peppers half way through
4. In a separate pan, reduce pineapple juice by 1/4. Add honey, soy sauce, ginger and coriander and reduce until sauce becomes thick. Serve sauce over the salmon.

Tomato Basil Soup

Serves a crowd!

Ingredients:

1 cup Fresh Basil, chopped
1 Large Yellow Onion, chopped
4 Celery Stalks, chopped
1/3 cup Dry Basil
2 Tbsp. Dry Thyme
2 Tbsp. Dry Oregano
1/4 cup Garlic, chopped

Continued

1/4 cup Brown Sugar
1/2 cup Sherry
1/2 cup Red Wine
1 gallon Vegetable Stock
3 Quarts (1 No. 10 Can) Stewed Tomatoes, drain liquid
3 Quarts (1 No. 10 Can) Tomato Sauce
Butter
Salt and Pepper to taste

Method:

Sauté onion and celery in butter until limp. Add fresh basil, cook 1 minute. Add dry herbs, mix well. Add sherry and red wine, brown sugar and garlic. Mix well and cook 5 minutes or until ingredients are fused well. Add vegetable stock, stewed tomatoes, and tomato sauce. Add salt and pepper to taste.

From Hotel Jeffery's Cooking Class
Spring Mix Salad with Red Wine, Honey Vinaigrette

Ingredients:

Large handful Spring Mix Salad Greens
4 Apple slices
1/2 cup Walnuts, halves or chopped
3 Tbsp. Butter
3 Tbsp. Brown Sugar
1/4 cup Red Onion, sliced rings
2 Tbsp. Gorgonzola Cheese, crumbled

Mix next ingredients together:
1 cup Red Wine Vinegar
1/2 cup Honey
2 Tbsp. Coriander
1/4 cup Olive Oil

Method:

In a sauce pan on low heat, add butter to melt, add walnuts, and coat, then add brown sugar, when melted take off of heat and let cool.
To assemble salad, add vinaigrette to spring mix, add apple slices on side of plate, sprinkle walnuts and cheese, top with red onion rings.

50

Painting of the original hotel by Leslie Rolfe

Groveland Hotel 1849
GROVELAND

*I*t has been called the Treasure of the Sierras. Located near the entrance to Yosemite, the Groveland Hotel is a masterpiece architecturally, historically, culturally and commercially. It has survived for 159 years, having ridden the winds of change from 1849 to the present and has retained its architectural integrity intact. It is one of the oldest buildings in Tuolumne County and is the largest adobe structure in Groveland. Classified as an example of the Monterey style of architecture, it represents one of the most outstanding gems of the Gold Rush era and is listed on the prestigious National Register of Historic Places.

51

Its place in the history of the central Sierra Nevada reflects a small town's colorful past. The first prospector to arrive in the area was James D. Savage, a member of Benjamin Wood's group of gold seekers in 1848. Savage began scouting out potential spots where the precious metal was hidden in nature's fertile earth. Winding his way into the area southeast of the Tuolumne River he set up camp in what became known as Savage Diggings. After his departure the camp was called Big Oak Flat. After a devastating fire in 1864, Big Oak Flat was destroyed and many of her buildings never rebuilt. First Garrote survived and in 1875 its name was changed to Groveland.

From the financial slump created after the demise of the Gold Rush, the Groveland Hotel would survive several pangs of boom and bust. In 1895 hard rock mining brought a new prosperity which lasted from 1895 to World War I. Fast upon the heels of that era came the arrival of the Hetch Hetchy project from 1914 to 1929. There were railroads to be built, equipment to be hauled and men to man the new jobs. And there was tourism. Groveland became known as the Gateway to Yosemite and her attraction for visitors has never waned. From stagecoaches to cars, visitors still head for one of the great wonders of the world—Yosemite National Park.

In 1929 another devastating era ensued as the Great Depression brought hard times to the area. After World War II, the Groveland Hotel again witnessed increased business—a hotel bar was added and it became a Greyhound bus stop. Then another slump followed in the 1950s. Many owners came and went, each one somewhat altering and changing the hotel and the grounds. For a while the hotel became offices for the Stanislaus National Forest. Then the property was sold in 1986 and went into a severe decline. Foreclosure and bankruptcy loomed when the owners could not meet their financial obligations. The hotel was an empty shell in derelict condition just a whisper away from being demolished. Fortunately, it turned out to be the storm before the dawn.

Enter Grover and Peggy Mosley. No one was more qualified to take on the reins of this enormous restoration project than

Peggy Mosley. As the first woman Executive Manager for Lockheed Missiles and Space Company, she also taught business courses at Evergreen Valley Junior College as well as financial management, computer and aviation classes for Embry-Riddle Aeronautical University, Moffett field Navy campus. Peggy has a private pilot's license and an instrument rating. From 1974 to 1983, she owned and operated Aero Systems, an aircraft rental and flight school in San Jose.

Upon her retirement in 1992, she discovered Pine Mountain Lake Airport and fell in love with the Groveland area. The Mosleys purchased a home nearby. Peggy then earned a real estate license and began looking around for a project which would interest her. In 1990 she noticed that the Groveland Hotel was desperately in need of a lot of T.L.C. and a major restoration. So began the rebirth of the hotel.

The day I visited, Peggy interrupted her very busy schedule to explain what was currently happening at the hotel. I learned something about the fine art of wine. For instance, the type of glass wine is served in can change its flavor. Peggy escorted me down narrow steps to the three wine cellars below and showed me over 12,000 bottles of vintage wine. The cellars' original 1849 adobe walls built by the Chinese are still intact.

The activities, which are offered by the hotel for visitors and guests, range from Innkeeper seminars; expeditions to Yosemite and the surrounding wilderness; special events, such as weddings; theater presented in a large outdoor rose-covered patio which seats over eighty people; mystery plays, and weekend Jazz festivals. There are also monthly activities marked on the calendar such as a Dickens Christmas, a Mark Twain Evening, and Romance packages. Special presentations are Patsy Cline, John Denver and Elvis Presley sing-alikes who liven up the evening.

If all of this is not enough, the coup de grace is the cuisine under the direction of executive chef Greg Lutes. The elegant dining room seats over fifty people and is responsible for serving a variety of delicacies which would delight the most discriminating taste. In 1997 the hotel hosted a James Beard 10th anniversary dinner, and it has been named one of the year's Ten Best Inns. The accolades don't stop there. In 2001 the Groveland Hotel earned their first *Wine Spectator* Award of Excellence. Television's popular host, Huell Howser, featured the hotel in one of his California's Gold television segments.

The Groveland Hotel has seventeen rooms which are magnificently decorated with European antiques, queen-size beds, private baths and there are three suites with fireplaces and Jacuzzi spa tubs.

And what would an historic hotel be without a resident ghost? "Lyle" resides in room No. 15. He came to the hotel in 1920, a prospector who was slightly eccentric. A miner yes, but he also liked sumptuous surroundings for his lodging come evening. It was said that he slept with a case of dynamite under his bed. With his passing in 1927, Lyle simply hung around. Warning: He doesn't like women's cosmetics. Many a female guest has noted that whatever jars of perfume or make-up she brings has a way of ending up on the floor or mysteriously finds another location.

When I asked Peggy if she had any special stories associated with the hotel, she listed a few of the famous visitors who have graced the establishment from U.S. Senator Barbara Boxer and actor John Belushi, to a Russian Cosmonaut.

Peggy informed me she had attended school with Elvis Presley in Memphis, Tennessee. There is even a group picture of Elvis and Peggy that she proudly displays. "Once his mother gave him that guitar," Peggy explained, "he just about slept with it." Her upbringing in Tennessee is one of the reasons the hotel offers cuisine with southern hospitality, Peggy's specialty. My taste buds were watering when she described her own favorite dish: chicken, of course, prepared in a variety of mouth-watering ways, followed by her own specially-prepared barbecued beans, cole slaw and a decadent chocolate molten mountain dessert served with ginger ice cream.

So, from stagecoach to Lear Jets, the Mosleys have turned an 1849 hotel into the 21st century masterpiece, capturing the flavor of the Old West with all the amenities. Entertainment, fine dining and luxurious accommodations, it's all right here in the heart of the central Sierra Nevada.

For more information, call the Groveland Hotel:
(209) 962-4000 or (800) 273-3314.

E-Mail: reservations@groveland.com

Website: www.groveland.com

Location: 18767 Main St. in Groveland, California

Mail: Groveland Hotel, P.O. Box 289, Groveland, CA 95321

How to get there:

From San Francisco and the Bay Area

Head east on Interstate 580. Near Tracy, merge on to I-205 East. Stay on I-205 until I-5 North. Take I-5 north for a very short distance. Take Highway 120 east toward Sonora/Yosemite. Remain on Hwy 120 east through Oakdale. Following signs to Yosemite's northern entrance, turn right at "Yosemite Junction." Stay on 120 east traveling up the hill into Groveland.

From the south

From Highway 99 in Merced, take Highway 140 east to Highway 49. Travel north to Moccasin Creek; Turn right to take Highway 120 east up the hill into Groveland.

From the north

From Highway 99 take Highway 120 through Escalon to Highway 120/108 to Oakdale. Go east to Yosemite Junction on Highway 49. Go south to Moccasin Creek and east on Highway 120 to Groveland.

Recipes: The Groveland Hotel

Roasted Vegetable Lasagna

Ingredients:

2 Red, Green or Yellow Bell Peppers, cut into 8 pieces each
1 Medium Onion, cut into 8 wedges
1 Large Zucchini, cut into 2-inch pieces (2 cups)
1 Eggplant, sliced into 1/8 inch thick slices
8 Roma Tomatoes, sliced 1/4 inch thick
1/4 cup Garlic, minced
1 pkg. (8 ounces) Whole Mushrooms, cut in half
2 Tbsp. Olive or Vegetable Oil
1/2 tsp. Ground Black Pepper
1/2 tsp. Ground White Pepper
2 tsp. Fresh Basil, chopped **or** 1/2 teaspoon dried basil leaves
9 Lasagna Noodles, uncooked
15 oz. Ricotta Cheese
1/2 cup Fresh Basil, chopped
1 Egg, slightly beaten
2 cups Provolone Cheese, shredded
1 cup Mozzarella Cheese, shredded

Method:

1. Heat oven to 425°.
2. Spray bottom and sides of jelly roll pan, 15 1/2 x 10 1/2 x 1 inch, with cooking spray.
3. Place bell peppers, onion, zucchini, eggplant, mushrooms, tomatoes, oil, garlic, salt, pepper and basil in large bowl; toss to coat. Spread vegetables in pan. Bake veggies uncovered about 30 minutes or until crisp-tender. Cool slightly.
4. Reduce oven temperature to 350°. Spray bottom and sides of a rectangular baking dish, 13x9x2 inches, with cooking spray. Cook and drain noodles as directed on package. Mix Ricotta Cheese and egg with basil. *Continued*

56

5. Place 3 noodles lengthwise in baking dish. Spread with half of the Ricotta mixture. Top with 2 cups vegetables and 1 cup of the Provolone cheese. Repeat layers, starting with noodles. Top with remaining 3 noodles and remaining vegetables. Sprinkle with Mozzarella cheese.

6. Bake uncovered 40 to 50 minutes or until hot in center and top until golden brown. Let stand 4 minutes before cutting. Cut into squares and serve with Rock Shrimp Mornay Sauce (Recipe below).

Rock Shrimp Mornay Sauce

Ingredients:

1 lb. Rock Shrimp
1 Shallot, minced
2 oz. Unsalted Butter
1 cup White Wine
1 cup Heavy Whipping Cream
1/4 cup Flour
1/2 cup Swiss Cheese
1/4 tsp. Nutmeg
1 tsp. Salt
1/2 tsp. White Pepper

Method:

In a small sauce pot on high heat, sauté the shrimp and shallot in the butter for 2 minutes. Add the white wine and reduce by two thirds. Remove from heat and whisk in the flour until smooth. Add the cream and bring to a simmer. Simmer 10 minutes stirring occasionally. Add remaining ingredients. Serve with Vegetable Lasagna.

Warm Ratatouille Salad with Fresh Goat Cheese
by Chef Greg Lutes

Ingredients:

1 Generous Tbsp. Extra-Virgin Olive Oil
2 Small Yellow or White Onions, chopped
2 Eggplants, cut into 1-inch cubes
4 Garlic Cloves, minced
2 Zucchini, cut into 1 inch cubes
2 Large Green, Red or Yellow Bell Peppers, cut in 1 inch pieces
8 to 10 Ripe Tomatoes, peeled, seeded and coarsely chopped
3 Fresh Thyme Sprigs
1 Fresh Rosemary Sprig
1 Dried Bay Leaf
1/2 tsp. Salt
1/2 tsp. Freshly ground pepper
1/4 cup Fresh Basil, minced
4 Tbsp. Balsamic Vinegar
4 cups Mixed Greens
8 oz. Fresh Goat Cheese

Method:

1. In a large, heavy saucepan or soup pot over medium heat, warm the olive oil. When it is hot, reduce the heat to medium-low, add the onions and sauté until translucent, about 2 minutes. Add the eggplant and garlic and sauté, stirring often, until the eggplant cubes are slightly softened, 3 to 4 minutes.

2. Add the zucchini and bell peppers and continue to sauté, stirring and turning, until softened, 4 to 5 minutes more. Add the tomatoes, thyme, rosemary, bay leaf, salt and pepper, and stir and turn for 2 to 3 minutes more.

3. Cover, reduce the heat to low and cook, stirring occasionally, until the vegetables are soft and somewhat blended together, about 40 minutes.

4. Stir in the basil and remove from the heat. Transfer to a mixing bowl and crumble the goat cheese into it, then toss in the mixed greens and the vinegar and serve while still warm.

Hotel Charlotte painting by Leslie Rolfe

Hotel Charlotte 1921
GROVELAND

When I visited the Hotel Charlotte in Groveland recently, I asked owner Lynn Upthagrove if she could relate any unusual stories about the hotel that occurred during its eighty-seven year history. She proceeded to tell me about Charlotte De Ferrari after whom the hotel was named. Born in Genoa, Italy in 1881, her family came to the gold fields when Charlotte was just sixteen.

By this time, the days of the '49 Gold Rush were long past. The area had gone through sporadic periods of boom and bust. With the building of the San Francisco Hetch Hetchy project, however, fame and fortune once again came to the Groveland area. Soon after young Charlotte's arrival tragedy stuck. Charlotte's father was killed in a mining accident. Young Charlotte rolled up her sleeves and went to work. As head of the family, she cooked for work crews, ranch hands and other settlers in order to earn a much needed income. Apparently she was successful. Soon thereafter she opened a restaurant where today's Iron Door Saloon is located. (Across the street from the Charlotte Hotel). She was a rarity in the community. There were very few female-headed businesses. In 1918, she looked around for a site to build a hotel, quite an undertaking for a young woman at that time. She found an old livery stable across the street and in 1921, purchased the Gem Saloon next door, annexing it to the hotel as a restaurant. Thus began a legend.

As Lynn explained to me, the hotel is really a family affair. It is a community center where the town's residents have come for years. Every Friday night the hotel acts like a social magnet and locals sit around telling their tall tales for visitors who happen to drop by. And they are entertained by the hotel's star attraction, Bob.

Who is Bob? Undeniably he is the center of attention. Bob is a thirteen year-old Terrier, about two feet long with soft brown eyes and the most winning personality you'll ever see in a canine. Bob was resting comfortably at the foot of a Persian rug in the hotel lobby when I asked Lynn what breed he was. She answered, "part Terrier, part attitude." I glanced back down at Bob to assess him more carefully.

"Would you like for him to do some tricks for you?" Lynn asked.

"Well sure," I answered.

Lynn told Bob to roll over. He did. "Crawl," she ordered. He did. "Sit up," she commanded. He did. "Give us a hand shake," she told him. And he did. Both the right and the left paw, by the way.

Well, all of this is all right. A lot of dogs do these things. Nothing all that unusual. But then Lynn turned to me and asked. "Would you like to hear Bob play the piano?"

Taken aback, I said, "Well, yes, I guess." I did not quite

believe what I heard. But I was game.

Lynn disappeared into the kitchen and a few minutes later, reappeared carrying several slices of bread.

"What would you like for him to play for you?" she asked me.

In total disbelief, I think I mumbled, "What about Silent Night?"

"OK," Lynn said.

She placed a slice of bread on the piano, and up jumped Bob, banging away at the keys as he stuffed the bread into his mouth. We all clapped. He had done his job well.

"What else would you like to hear?"

"Well, what about Joy to the World?"

"OK," Lynn replied and up again Bob flew on the keyboard, banging away at the keys as he wolfed down another piece of bread.

"I see Bob has quite a repertoire."

"Oh, yes," Lynn replied. "He can go on all night."

Bob had not finished. Yes, he had an encore up his "sleeve." Lynn asked him to go home. He jumped down from the piano and walked to his home, a large wine keg situated behind the counter where an oval had been cut out for a door. There he charged into his sleeping quarters smothered with blankets and peered back at us. Was he laughing, or winking at me or just pleased in having entertained all of us to our satisfaction?

Lynn explained that all the children who stay at the hotel always mention Bob and how much they love him. The hotel does, by the way, have a pet room just for those special pets guests have brought with them.

Note: Bob passed away in 2008. His colorful successor is Goose. I was informed that Goose, the hotel dog, ran for mayor and came in a "very close second." He has earned the title of 1st Deputy Honorary Mayor of Groveland. Interview with Christi Kirk, September 2, 2008.

For more information, call Hotel Charlotte: (209) 962-6455
Web Page: www.hotelcharlotte.com
E-mail: HotelCharlotte@aol.com
Location: 18736 Main St., Groveland, California (Highway 120)
Mail: Hotel Charlotte, P.O. Box 787, Groveland, CA 95321

How to get there:
From Highway 99 and Merced, take Highway 140 east, turn north on Highway 49 to Moccasin Creek, go east on Highway 120 to Groveland.

From Sacramento take Highway 16 to Highway 49, go south to Moccasin Creek, then east on Highway 120 to Groveland; or take Highway 99 south to Highway 120 through Escalon and Oakdale. Turn south on Highway 49 to Moccasin Creek, travel east on Highway 120 to Groveland.

Recipes from the Hotel Charlotte

Chicken Jerusalem
(The Hotel Charlotte's best selling item on the menu)
Serves 4

Ingredients:

2 Boneless Chicken Breasts, trimmed
1 Tbsp. Butter
1/2 tsp. Fresh Garlic, chopped
1 cup Button Mushrooms
1/2 cup canned Artichoke Hearts, quartered
1/2 cup Sherry
1/4 cup Heavy Cream
Salt and Pepper to taste.

Method:

Lightly pound chicken breasts to uniform 1/2 inch thick pieces. Cut each in half. Melt 1 Tbsp. butter in a sauce pan. Dredge chicken pieces in flour and sauté in butter until cooked through. Add chopped garlic, mushrooms and the artichoke hearts. Sauté together for 5 minutes. Add other ingredients to pan. Reduce at high heat for 5 minutes or until reduced by half.

Argentine Sauce (Chimi-Churri)

Ingredients:

1 Tbsp. Fresh Garlic, chopped
2 Tbsp. Fresh Italian Parsley, chopped
1/2 tsp. Fresh Ground Black Pepper
1/2 tsp. Salt
1/2 cup Extra Virgin Olive Oil

Mix all of the ingredients together, use as a marinade or topping for grilled meats and chicken.

63

Sicilian Pasta

Ingredients:

1 Tbsp. Olive Oil
1 Tbsp. Fresh Garlic, chopped
1 Tbsp. Sun Dried Tomatoes, soaked in water for 20 minutes and sliced thin.
1/4 tsp. Pepper Flakes
1/4 cup White Wine
1/4 cup Asparagus, parboiled and cut in bite-size pieces
2 cups Bow-tie Pasta, cooked
Salt and Pepper, to taste
Fresh Parmesan Cheese, grated

Method:

Sauté garlic in olive oil until just starting to bubble; add sun dried tomatoes and pepper flakes, sauté for 1 minute. Add the white wine and simmer for an additional minute. Add asparagus, pasta, salt and pepper to taste. Toss until well blended and hot throughout. Serve with fresh Parmesan cheese.

This delicious dish is Vegetarian. If you want to make it heartier, you can add spicy sausage or chicken.

From
Miners 49er Cookbook by Robert Stahl - 1970

Sonofabitch Stew

*This infamous concoction got its beginning
from the early cowpuncher's grub.*

Ingredients:

Into the chosen pot goes each and every item that is
unwanted elsewhere. A good amount of shredded beef and
a fair amount of vegetables, except for potatoes and onions
—lots of these. Some Skillygalee to moisten whatever else
is lying around loose.[1]

Method:

Look around and be sure that nothing real important
is missing and let 'er rip.

---

[1] Skillygalee was made by soaking hardtack in water and then
frying it in lard. Skillygalee was also eaten by soldiers during
the Civil War.

Jamestown Hotel in Jamestown, California

Jamestown Hotel 1858
JAMESTOWN

*T*he Jamestown Hotel is all about cuisine—superb cuisine. The hotel's new owners, Brian and Dawn Solomon, have only owned the hotel for a short time, but their restaurant, Solomon's Landing (currently closed), has already earned the title of one of the very best dining spots in the Mother Lode.

Yes the hotel, like all the hotels in the communities along historic Highway 49, has lots of history buried in its walls and tons of stories to tell dating from the golden days of 1848 and 1849. Overnight thousands of men came from throughout the world to seek their fortune flocking to the

66

hills of the central Sierra. They were adventurers and perhaps daydreamers, but the dream was simply too good not to be true. Some indeed did strike it rich and found their pot of gold at the end of the rainbow. Their tales fill the annals of the Mother Lode with their daring and audacious can-do spirit. That spirit still lingers. Geologists tell us that only a small percentage of the gold hidden in "them thar hills" has ever been extracted. And who knows, with the price of gold soaring, it could all happen again.

In the meantime, Jamestown simply reels with the feel and flavor of those bygone days. A recent tourist came to town and was shocked to find the entire main street covered in dirt. "My gosh," he said. "This place is really authentic, they haven't even paved it!" The impressed young visitor later learned that a film crew had been shooting a movie in town and had covered the street with dirt to re-enact a scene. Oh well, for a moment he witnessed what Jamestown was like before the world rushed in. Dreams die hard. In Jamestown and much of the Mother Lode, however, there is still a lot to see of that world of the Old West.

For example, on a recent visit to the Jamestown Hotel, I simply had to walk up to the balcony on the second floor and take a peek down Main Street. To be truthful, I couldn't help but wonder what it must have been like when young women dressed in all their finery were luring men upstairs for the night. Jamestown was, after all, noted for its bordellos where many a young "soiled dove" draped over a hotel balcony, yelled at miners passing by to "come up for a spell."

Across the street the old Emporium, once a thriving mercantile store, has been recently restored and looks magnificent. The street still meanders slightly and store after store bears the mark of another era. Tourists can even mine for gold and a store next to the Emporium guarantees they will find gold for $5.

When I sat down with Dawn Solomon recently, I asked her what drew her to the Mother Lode. She and her husband Brian had a restaurant in Cabo San Lucas, Mexico which they still own. Their specialty was fish. While visiting the Mother Lode they simply fell in love with it. Wanting a simpler life style and also hoping their daughter could grow up in an area that was less hectic, they found the Jamestown Hotel. It was love at first sight.

The hotel has eight rooms, all with private baths and some also have parlors as well. It gives guests a lot more space to sit around and chat. All the rooms are richly decorated with antiques, and the guests are also served an ample breakfast with home-made quiche or Belgian waffles, if they prefer.

Dawn's specialty is wine. Her book, *An Insider's Guide To Wine Tasting,* will turn any amateur wine lover into a connoisseur. She offers special wine tasting classes once a month from appetizers to dessert accompanied with the appropriate choice of a variety of wines that bring out the flavors and aromas of the courses served.

Of course the hotel has its resident ghost, Mary Rose who usually shows up in room No. 7, but has also been seen by others, strolling in the hall. Once, when cleaning out the basement, one of the employees found an old time doll. Eerily, it kept saying "Mommy" over and over. In the dark, with its glass eyes shinning, it was just too much to bear, so the doll was thrown away. The employee said she could still hear it crying, "Mommy."

For more information call the Jamestown Hotel: (209) 984-3902 (800) 205-4901
Website: jamestownhotel.com
E-mail: info@JamestownHotel.com
Location and mail: Jamestown Hotel, 18153 Main Street, Jamestown, CA 95327

How to get there:
From the south: take Highway 99 to Merced, go north on Highway J59 through Snelling, stay on J59, take Highway 108/120 east to Jamestown.

From the west or north:
From Manteca on Highway 99, go east on Highway 120 through
Escalon and Oakdale, stay on Highway 108/120 east to Jamestown.

Brian Solomon sat down with me and explained his love of
seafood. Food is a passion for him and the restaurant menu bears
that out. He gave me the following recipes.

Recipes from Jamestown Hotel

Oysters Rockefeller

Ingredients:

    12 Oysters on the half shell
    4 Cloves Garlic, chopped med. coarse
    Clarified Butter or Light Olive Oil
    Kosher Salt
    Black Pepper, fresh ground
    Handful of Fresh Spinach, finely chopped
    Handful of Button Mushrooms, finely chopped
    Mozzarella Cheese
    Parmesan Cheese

Method:

1. Shuck and drain the oysters in their shells, the deeper bottom shell
is rinsed and reserved for baking.
2. Take four cloves of garlic and chop medium coarse.
3. Take a big handful of fresh spinach and a handful of button mushrooms which have been chopped fine.
4. In a small sauté pan, sauté the garlic in clarified butter or a light
olive oil just until it turns brown.
5. Then add spinach and mushrooms and grated mozzarella cheese.
Stir. Add a pinch of kosher salt and a pinch of black pepper. Stir in pan
until bubbling. Put one tablespoon of mixture on top of oysters on the

half shell spread fresh grated Parmesan cheese on top of oysters. Bake in pre-heated 400° oven for 15 to 20 minutes until golden brown. Remove. Cool 2 or 3 minutes, then serve immediately.

Granola

Ingredients:

> 2 Tubs (18 oz. ea.) Quaker Rolled Oats - not quick or instant
> 2 cups Sliced Almonds
> 1 cup Sesame Seeds
> 3 Tbsp. Cinnamon
> 1 Tbsp. Salt
> Pinch of Ground Cloves
>
> 1 cup Honey
> 1 cup Maple Syrup
> 1 cup Canola Oil
> 1/4 cup Vanilla
>
> 2 cups Dried Cranberries or Raisins

Method:

Combine dry ingredients in a large bowl, except cranberries. Place wet ingredients in a microwave safe dish and microwave for 2 minutes to allow easier mixing and coverage of dry ingredients. Combine the wet and dry ingredients in the large bowl and mix until dry ingredients are all covered.

Place mixture on baking sheets and spread thin. Bake at 300° until gold brown, stirring frequently (approximately 20 to 30 minutes). Remove from oven and let cool completely. Add the dried cranberries or raisins and transfer to a storage container.

From
Miners 49er Cookbook by Robert Stahl - 1970

Red Flannel Hash

Out of pure orneriness, a member of the fair sex ground up the better portion of her true love's red flannel long johns and placed the results midst the meat hash that the culprit was preparing to serve all takers at his commercial eating house. The results were sensational and great demands for "more of that bright red hash," they cried. In attempting to duplicate the hash, the proprietor failed since he did not know the "special ingredient." The enterprising chef grated fresh beets and behold — bright red hash.

Ingredients:

    3 Fresh Red Beets, grated
    1 cup Potatoes, diced
    1 Medium Onion, chopped
    1 Can Tinned Beef, 8 oz.
    2 Eggs
    Salt & Pepper

Method:

    Put 'er all together and fry slow.

Note: Author takes no responsibility for anyone crazy enough to try to make this recipe.

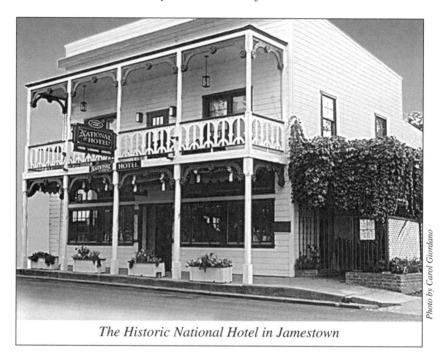

Photo by Carol Giordano

The Historic National Hotel in Jamestown

National Hotel 1859
JAMESTOWN

*A*fter James Marshall's discovery of gold in January 1848, the greatest mass migration in the history of our nation descended upon the central Sierra. Every language was heard, every profession represented. The impact was staggering. Unlike the migration from Europe to America from the 15th to the 19th centuries, this exodus was from the east to the far west. No one could have imagined that such tumultuous change would occur in so short a space of time. The West, henceforth, would continue to alter older, more traditional ways, injecting a sense of adventure, change and inventiveness into our current values. California has cast a long shadow and continues to re-shape the American character even today.

Following the trail of those first '49ers, the Mother Lode

still lures modern day arm-chair adventurers—tourists from all over the world who want to relive that first rush to riches. From Coloma and James Marshall's discovery of gold along the American River in 1848, the would-be miners scattered all over the Sierras. One of the first stops along that trail was Wood's Creek in Jamestown. The miners hung up temporary tent shelters and headed for the creeks and rivers to pan for gold. Among the first to arrive was Colonel George James, a San Francisco lawyer. Part businessman, part scallywag, he believed that what the gold seekers needed was not just a pick and shovel, canned beans and coffee, but more—the stuff that dreams are made of— the promise of wealth and the lavish ambiance to go with it.

The Colonel put up an imposing tent which housed a hotel, a bar and a speculative mining operation. He topped it all off with ample servings of ice cold champagne which must have tickled the appetite of men whose fiery disposition was eager to fulfill the riches that El Dorado promised. While they exploited the earth, James exploited their pocketbooks.

At first the miners loved James. As long as the champagne flowed, they decided to name the new community after him— Jimtown or Jamestown. For men whose only entertainment had been quiet evenings at home around a cozy fire reading passages from the Bible, adjustments would take time to separate the rascals and no accounts from men who took ethics and morality seriously. This was a new world they had never encountered before. Luck changed on the roll of the dice, or the turn of a card, or the broad smile of a pretty girl when a man's pockets were full of gold dust. It was an unstable, mobile society where the velocity of change was unsettling. Old traditions and morals were cast aside with reckless abandon.

James proved to be one of the less than honorable rascals. When his mining speculation failed, he slipped quietly out of town, leaving his creditors high and dry. The miners were awakened to a new reality, a reality that was hard to swallow. They were rip-roaring mad so they decided to change the name of their town from Jamestown to American Camp. Later the name was changed back to Jamestown or Jimtown for short.

In spite of early setbacks, the community continued to

grow and reached its gold frenzy around 1852 when the population numbered over 17,000 people. Gambling houses were dens of iniquity where drinking and loose women testified to a new kind of life. Hotels were enormously profitable and the first place a stranger could go to find a friend. In 1859 the Europa was built on Main Street. Like the other hotels, it had a long balcony where ladies of the evening could drape themselves over the railing, calling to the patrons downstairs anxious to spend their winnings. It was one of the rare cases where architectural design proved extremely well suited to the profession of prostitution. It is said that "women made the Europa." Jamestown had a reputation to match that claim. It was known as a lively red-light district where brothels provided welcome relief to the men exhausted from their work in the diggings. Even if they "lost their shirt," they could always return to their claims for another try at lady luck. Hope reigned eternal in paradise, and every man believed that a new day would turn over the find of a lifetime. Jamestown kept this reputation as a lively "hangout" for women of ill-repute and even legalized gambling until Governor Edmund G. (Pat) Brown cleaned out the place in the 1950s.

The Europa later became The National Hotel owned by Mrs. Angelina Carboni and Joe Graziani. It burned many times and in the 1880s its wooden frame was replaced. In 1928 the structure was built of concrete which has remained to this day. In 1975 Steve Willey purchased the hotel and continues to renovate and operate it today.

When I first visited Jamestown in the late 1950s, the town was still very lively. It had the reputation as *the* place to dine. There were several hotels which offered excellent fare: the Willow, Jamestown Hotel, The National Hotel and several Chinese restaurants. I remember strolling down the streets where antique shops and beautiful old Victorian homes drew wide-eyed tourists like bees to honey. My family always headed for The National Hotel for dinner. The food was superb and the hotel was like taking a magic carpet ride back to the flavor of the '49ers era. It seemed as if nothing had ever changed. One could savor the passage of time without losing the authenticity of the past.

Almost fifty years have elapsed since that first visit and little has changed. The old 1859 bar that came around the Cape Horn is still there. During all the many fires that have necessitated restoration of the hotel, the bar was always saved. I can almost picture it now—firefighters fighting to save at any cost what really mattered—the place where they could hang out and share stories downed with the elixir of the gods. And the bar is a work of art. Across it hangs a beautiful rope of blue glass made in Italy. It was given to the hotel by workmen who appreciated working at the hotel. If you look closely, every other bead of glass looks like it has the bubbly still residing within it.

Liza, the local bartender, told me that *Back to the Future* star "Doc"—Christopher Lloyd's favorite drink is still waiting for him when he drops by—Mcallan's Scotch. The National Hotel remains home to many film and television legends.

I retired to the dining room to have lunch and feasted on caramelized French Onion Soup with homemade sourdough bread, followed by a Greek Salad sprinkled with lots of Feta Cheese, Greek Olives, onions and a pungent dressing. I completed my lunch with a refreshing cup of orange sherbet

The dining room seats about eighty and there is a vine-covered patio outside which seats another forty-five people. The walls are richly covered in satinesque wallpaper and dark paneling. The lighting may be electric, but the beautiful chandeliers remind you of old fashioned gas lighting. There are old doorknobs which, at 5' 9," I have to bend down to reach. Framed pictures of guests from another era hang on the deep magenta walls.

As I was having lunch my waitress, Lisa (not the bartender), introduced me to another town character, Clinton, a white-haired old timer who once worked at the hotel. He is retired and hangs around as a kind of personal greeter. He comes by every day and asks people, "Got any mail? I'll take it to the post office." He bowed to me and we shook hands. Time stands still here; the pace definitely slows down.

When I finished lunch I meandered upstairs. Each of the National's nine rooms has a private bath and is decorated with antiques that befit the era. And, of course, there is room No. 10. That is Flo's room—the friendly resident ghost. Many guests who have stayed at the National Hotel talk about Flo and the hotel has testimonials to her comings and goings.

The hotel offers a continental breakfast and, on Sunday mornings, brunch comes with champagne. The hotel is pet-friendly. Dogs are definitely allowed and there are treats just for them. There are plenty of tour arrangements to choose from, including local theaters and visits to the Mother Lode's many attractions with special packages on Thanksgiving, New Year's Eve, Valentine's Day, Saint Patrick's Day, Easter and Christmas.

For more information call the National Hotel: (209) 984-3446

Reservations: (800) 894-3446

E-mail: info@national-hotel.com

Web page: www.national-hotel.com

Location: 18183 Main Street, Jamestown, California

Mail: National Hotel, P.O. Box 502, Jamestown, CA 95327

How to get there:

From Fresno...
Take Highway 99 north to Merced. Then take Highway J59 north to Highway 108, Turn east to Jamestown and Sonora.

From Sacramento and Stockton...
Take Highway 99 south to Manteca. Take Highway 108/120 east through Escalon and Oakdale to Jamestown.

Favorite Recipes from the National Hotel

Raspberry Vinaigrette
Makes 1 pint (16 1 oz. Servings.)

Ingredients:

1 Large Egg
3/4 cup Granulated Sugar
16 oz. (2 cups) Salad Oil
1/4 cup Red Wine Vinegar
1/4 cup Raspberries (puréed and strained)

Method:

Combine egg and vinegar in blender. Slowly add 2 cups salad oil. Add sugar and raspberries. Mix well.

Crème Brûlée

Ingredients:

2 cups Whole Milk
3 cups Half and Half Cream
4 cups Sugar
2 Vanilla Beans
18 Egg Yolks

continued

77

Method:

Heat oven to 350 degrees

1. Separate egg yolks and place in a large bowl and stir.

2. In another large bowl, combine the half and half and the milk.

3. Mix in the sugar until it is dissolved.

4. Heat mixture in a sauce pan and add the two vanilla beans.

5. Heat milk mixture to a simmer. Remove from heat.

6. Remove vanilla beans from milk mixture, place on a flat surface and split lengthwise. Then, using the dull edge of a knife, scrape out the inside of the beans. Rinse the bean pods in the warm mixture and discard the pods. Mix the scrapings from the bean pod into the milk.

7. Gradually add the warm milk mixture to the egg yolks, mixing constantly.

8. The mixture should then be ladled into 4 ounce Pyrex custard cups. Then place the cups in a 4-inch deep baking pan, in a half inch of water. Place baking pan on stove top and bring water to a boil. Then turn off heat and immediately cover pan with aluminum foil.

9. Carefully place pan in oven at 350° for 30 minutes. *Do not over-cook*, as this is crucial to the texture of the finished product. Allow the Crème Brûlée to sit for at least 5 minutes before serving.

Halibut with Shrimp Paté and Apricot Glaze
Serves 8

Ingredients:

    2 lbs. (32 oz.) Halibut
    1/2 Pound (2 sticks) Butter
    9 oz. Small Bay Shrimp, cooked and peeled
    1 Pkg. Phyllo Dough
    1 Tbsp. Lemon Juice

Method:

1. Cut Halibut into 4 ounce pieces

2. Melt the butter and skim off fat.

3. Combine shrimp and lemon juice in blender. Purée and strain off excess fluid by pressing in a towel.

4. Unfold fresh Phyllo dough and remove two thin pieces.

5. Drizzle with melted butter, then fold 2 edges toward the middle and drizzle again.

6. Place halibut at one end and cover top with shrimp paté.

7. Roll halibut in dough, folding in the edges to seal. Brush entire roll with butter and place on a buttered parchment paper.

8. Refrigerate thoroughly before handling.

9. Bake at 350° for 15 minutes, until brown.
Serve with Apricot Glaze (below).

Apricot Glaze

Ingredients:

    2 cups Apricot Halves
    3 ounces Brandy
    1 cup packed Brown Sugar

Blend until smooth. Heat and serve over Halibut.

Photo by Patty Wright

Royal Carriage Inn, Jamestown, California

Photo by Patty Wright

Royal Carriage Inn
Formerly The Royal Hotel 1922
JAMESTOWN

*T*he Royal Hotel, as it was first known, was built in 1922 by Royal H. Rushing. Local advertisements touted the Royal as being luxurious in every detail. I was able to find the original article in our local library on Greenley Road which appeared in the *Union Democrat* August 12, 1922:

"Jamestown's Fine Modern Fireproof Hotel Will Be Opened this Saturday Evening With An Informal Reception During Which The General Public Will be Privileged To Inspect It. Jamestown can proudly boast of having the most modern up-to-date hotel anywhere in the interior of the

State; indeed, the equal in point of substantiality of construction, beauty of finish and comfort of equipment, of many in the larger centers of population.

One of the best assets of any community is a good hotel and this has been supplied in the Mother Lode by R.H. Rushing, a Tuolumne County born and reared boy, who in the face of much discouragement persisted in making a heavy investment in the structure, hereby expressing his abiding faith in the future of his native county and the Jamestown district in particular. He was imbued with the feeling that the attractions offered the homeseeker, the traveling man and the tourist would bring a patronage that would pay a handsome interest on the twenty and odd thousand dollars required to construct and furnish the hostelry.

The structure is of reinforced concrete, two stories with basement, and covers a ground space 34x80 feet. It's adorned in front by a balcony and a rear porch of the same dimension. The lobby is 15x26 feet, covered with linoleum and furnished with massive leather easy chairs and lounge. Overseeing the fireplace is a large oil painting of Mr. Rushing. A wide stairway leads to the upper story into a spacious hallway seven and a half feet wide, running the full length of the building, and is illuminated by five large globed incandescent lamps. The building was wired and electrical fixtures installed by the Tuolumne County Electric Power and Light Company. The rooms are light and airy and cheerful in wall effects and stained woodwork and the cleverness of the architect is shown in the economy of floor space. There are eight porcelain bathtubs of the latest patterns and an equal number of toilets.

A space on the ground floor to the left of the lobby facing the street forms a large dining room. There is a large kitchen conveniently arranged and with all proper connections in the rear. It will be noted by the above half-tone that the plate glass front which is to adorn this portion of the structure is not yet in place.

...Mr. Rushing and the real manager of Hotel Royal, his charming and excellent wife, have been prevailed upon to

open the hostelry this Saturday evening, when an informal reception will be held between 8 and 10 o'clock and to which a cordial invitation is extended to the general public to be present."

Thus, as stated in the article, did the Royal Hotel, or today's Royal Carriage Inn, make its debut in Jamestown. The day I visited, I found the lobby particularly inviting, with a beautiful candelabra, a large picture of Mr. Rushing over the fireplace and comfortable antique furniture.

There are eleven rooms, a banquet room with a cozy fireplace and a bookcase/library. Guests are served breakfast which is ample: bacon, ham, sausage and eggs or pancakes and lots of piping hot coffee to drink. The entire hotel is furnished in a 1920s craftsman style which lends warmth to the establishment.

For more information call the Royal Carriage Inn: (209) 984-5271

Fax: 209 984-1675

E-mail: info@royalcarriageinn.com

Web page: www.royalcarriageinn.com

Location: 18239 Main Street in Jamestown, Calif.

Mail: Royal Carriage Inn, 18239 Main St., Jamestown, CA 95327

How to get there:

From Fresno...
Take Highway 99 north to Merced. Then take Highway J59 north through Snelling to Highway 108, Turn east to Jamestown.

From Sacramento and Stockton...
Take Highway 99 south to Manteca. Take Highway 108/120 east through Escalon and Oakdale to Jamestown.

1021 The Willow Hotel, Jamestown, California.

The old Hotel Willow 1856
Today's Willow Saloon & Steakhouse 1922
JAMESTOWN

*S*ally Hamilton's well-researched book on the Willow hotel begins thus: "Whether I believe in the ghosts or not, they were my reason for starting my research on the Hotel Willow."[1] Sally's nine-year old son, Brandon, was intrigued by the stories he had heard about apparitions that supposedly went "Boo" in the night and wanted to know if the hauntings were true. His mother had worked there for more than twenty years, so she had heard just about every yarn that passed through the old walls of the Willow. She spent the next several years uncovering every article, every story, chasing

---

[1] Sally Hamilton, <u>Hotel Willow, Vol.1: Legends of the Hotel Willow Series</u>. (Book-em Publications, Jamestown, California,1995). Note: I have quoted freely from her book with Sally's permission.

down leads and interviewing people. The results are well worth reading.

One of the stories that interested her was an article written after the fire on July 21, 1985. That incident made headlines all over the world. There was even a letter from a famed parapsychologist, Nick Nocerino. Sally became more intent on researching the hotel and its supposed ghosts when she noted that an earlier fire occurred in 1975.[2] Fires were not new to Gold Rush hotels. Every decade, it seemed, a fire ravaged the old towns and the Willow was no exception.

But it was not only fires Sally found, but murders as well. A Mrs. Ratto had been shot by her husband in 1928 at the Willow. Headlines read: *Jamestown Startled by Double Tragedy that Ended Lives of Two*. There were also two hangings at the hotel where, on consecutive nights, two total strangers took their own lives.

To put it mildly, the hotel has had quite a history. It began life when a Portuguese emigrant, John Pereira, came to California from Louisiana in 1849 to what was then known as Georgetown.[3] Today, if old timers remember that name at all, they refer to it as the north end of Jamestown

John set up a tent where the Willow now stands. He was apparently successful as a gold miner and businessman. From his tent he bought gold, then sold groceries and supplies. Just across from that early spot there was bullfighting. Remember, California was populated mainly by Mexicans and Sonora was founded by men who came from Sonora, Mexico. One of their favorite sports was bullfighting.

In 1851 both Georgetown and the bordering community of American Camp agreed to combine and return to the original name of the town—Jamestown.

By 1855 Pereira realized the area needed a hotel which he built (rumored to be built on top of several mines) and called it

---

[2]Ibid. p. 42.

[3]This was my first introduction to the name Georgetown. Most sources discuss Jimtown as the town's first name, then Jamestown.

the Jamestown Hotel. He later changed the name to Hotel Willow due to the beautiful old Willow trees which adorned the front of the hotel. In 1863 the Hotel Willow burned. Thirty-three years passed before Pereira decided he needed to replace the shanties he had constructed on the site with a first-rate hotel.

There were certainly good reasons for rebuilding. The years 1896-1897 experienced an incredible growth in Jamestown. The Sierra Railroad had been built and with the influx of new residents and visitors a need was created for more accommodations. It was time to resurrect the Willow. This time the hotel would have twenty-two rooms, baths, a barber shop, a restaurant and other modern conveniences, including electricity in 1898.[4]

In October 1898, Pereira's pride and joy was leased to a Mr. Stone. The Sonora papers hailed the Willow as a beautifully and sumptuously furnished hotel, second only to the Victoria Hotel in Sonora.

There were more additions to the hotel. Rates increased from one dollar to two dollars a day. Another change was the beautiful bar purchased in 1897 in San Francisco and installed in 1898.

In 1899 the Willow was sold by John Pereira for the princely sum of $4,000 to Frank Mayer. There were, by this time, several lodging and tenement cottages in the rear.

Since the turn of the 20th century, the hotel has had its share of owners as well as distinguished guests. None other than the Western outlaw, Bat Masterson, signed the hotel register in 1901. That same year President McKinley signed in on May 24, 1901. Just four months later (September 6, 1901) our twenty-fifth president would be shot.[5]

Today, the Willow is owned by Kevin Mooney. It has survived dozens of fires and had a major restoration in 1975

---

[4]There was also the famous Nevills Hotel in Jamestown built by the same man who built the Victoria Hotel, now the Sonora Days Inn.

[5]The hotel register was purchased in 1961, shortly after Mary Stevenson (Mary Endicott) bought the Willow. She was shopping in an antique store and there she located one of the Willow's ledgers. Today that ledger is the only one known to exist and is in the hands of Sally Hamilton.

which won a Gold Nugget Award from the Tuolumne County Historical Society at its Annual Lamplight Dinner. Alas, the hotel burned again just three years later in 1978 and was never replaced. Only the restaurant and bar remain today.

And what about the ghosts that Sally went searching for? She writes that just before the 1978 fire a short little guy, whose identity was unknown, appeared at one of the doors. Shortly after the fire, Nick Nocerino, the longest practicing parapsychologist in California came to the Willow with a six-member entourage. They investigated the charred remains for four days and ascertained that nine distinct types of spirits were contacted. Four of them were convinced to leave, the others had no place to go. They also predicted that more fires were in the Willow's future.[6]

As it so happened, in 1981 another fire did occur. Luckily the bar was still open and the fire was extinguished before much damage had taken place. A few months later in 1982, when the Willow was closed for remodeling, some youngsters started a fire. They then ran down Main Street and reported that they saw smoke at the Willow. Thanks to quick action, fire damage was limited to a small part of the hotel.

In October 1992, a large celebration of the Willow's 130th birthday took place. Today, the restaurant and the memories of the old hotel are nearing 145 years of age and so far, so good.

---

[6]Former owner, Mary Endicott, claims the ghost stories are, absolutely, not true. She and her husband, Bill, owned the Willow from 1961 to 1971. Interview, July 26, 2007.

For information on the Willow Steakhouse: (209) 984-3998
Location: Willow and Main Street, Jamestown, California

Photo by Carol Giordano

Sonora Days Inn in 2008

Sonora (Days) Inn 1896
SONORA

*T*he Sonora Inn Hotel (Sonora Days Inn) has been a landmark in Sonora since it was built as the Victoria Hotel in 1896. But in a unique way, the man who built it was such an eccentric character, one has to question which was the most notable—the man or the hotel.

Captain William Alexander Nevills was acerbic, irascible and just plain difficult to get along with. In today's vernacular, we would classify him as a Type A personality—someone who shoots from the hip. He sued almost everyone with whom he did business and he shed wives and acquired mistresses with charm and aplomb. His scandalous behavior was a newspaperman's dream. But for all the notoriety, Nevills remains to this day, an enduring memory of Mother Lode history.

His life was a series of adventures beginning in Canada. He became a sailor, a miner and an entrepreneur, but mostly, Nevills was a risk-taker. His acutely sensitive nose for a good deal consistently paid off. He learned mining in the Arizona territory when he fought Mescalero Apaches and endured heat that reached 120 degrees in the shade. Barely out of his teens, his first investment of $1,200 turned into $150,000 in gold. While the iron was hot, he sold a half interest in his bonanza for $250,000.

By 1884 Nevills was in Angels Camp. He heard about a mine in Jamestown called the Rawhide. The mine, however, had a terrible reputation. Even Mark Twain took pleasure in noting the fate of the men who tried to work it. By the time Nevills entered the picture, the Rawhide was an old and neglected mine, long since played out and worthless. At least that's what everyone thought. Nevills had one of his hunches. He bought the "worthless" Rawhide for the rock bottom price of $16,000. The local townspeople had quite a laugh. A city slicker, they said, has bought the Rawhide. What a laugh! Nevills would, as it turned out, have the last laugh.

The young, resourceful go-getter rolled up his sleeves and went to work. The Rawhide would, under his astute management, produce over six million dollars in gold during the county's second Gold Rush (up to 1909). He followed that success with yet another treasure trove, the App Mine. By this time Nevills' reputation had grown so much, it was said that he had the Midas Touch.

Nevills never looked back. He began investing in grape vineyards, a stock farm in Fresno, and numerous ranches in the area. He turned his attention to stagecoaches, hotels and utility companies. The effect on Tuolumne County was significant. Nevills' luck created a tremendous new era of prosperity in the small county whose best days had, everyone believed, long since passed. He literally started Tuolumne County's second

Gold Rush.

He was also a man used to the comforts and conveniences of San Francisco and his favorite hotel, The Palace. When he stayed in Tuolumne County on business, he had to "rough it" in poor accommodations that were not up to his usual fine taste or standards. Hotels were often crowded to the roof top and frequently guests were compelled to seek sleeping rooms in private homes. The story goes that he was so upset one day with the service in a local hotel, he vowed to build a hotel of his own just to get even.

With his typical savvy and energy, Nevills looked around for a project in which he could direct his enormous talent. The best central location in Sonora was the corner of South Washington Street and Stockton Road. It had been a focal point since 1849 when the first Mexican miners came to town and laid out a central plaza. Later, the Lafayette Restaurant and the American Bath House were built on the site. When fire destroyed much of downtown Sonora on June 18, 1852, the Mexican plaza was eliminated by the City Trustees in favor of a uniform, Americanized main street one block long and eighty feet wide. It was named Washington Street.

In the spring of 1895, Nevills paid $16,500 for the corner plus two adjacent lots. The hotel that Nevills constructed would be the finest hostelry in the central Sierra Nevada, befitting the name the town had acquired during the Gold Rush: "Queen of the Southern Mines."

Stonemasons Cavallero and Ventre were hired. Local slate, quarried from Tuolumne County's own hills, was used throughout. The main building was three stories high and contained a large dining room, a saloon, a kitchen, and parlors. The hotel contained forty-eight rooms, earning the title of the largest hotel east of San Francisco. There was a long balcony which stretched the entire length of the facade where people could sit in the evening watching the passing parade. The basement boasted of having a wine cellar stocked with the best wines, a bakery, laundry and meat lockers. There was a beautiful courtyard containing flowers and tropical plants, their fragrance wafting throughout the hotel, delighted the guests.

Victoria Hotel during construction 1896-1897

Inside the building, art was hung everywhere. Frescoes, paintings and tintings were in the hands of the well-known firm of Blanchard and Shell of Stockton, under the direct supervision of Mrs. Delia Nevills. The finest redwood and mahogany woods covered the interior walls and stairs. Magnificent gas and electric lights hung from the vaulted ceilings and furnishings were lavish.

Menus featured the very best the area could provide. A popular delicacy was oysters, in any style. Rooms cost $ .50, $ .75 and $1.00 a day on the European plan. Five stagecoaches a day roared up to the front entrance delivering their arrivals with great fanfare and anticipation. Nevills named his new venture The Victoria Hotel, after Queen Victoria of England. It would cost an astonishing $100,000 to build, but it attracted a wide array of patrons.

Victoria Hotel (Sonora Days Inn) in 1927—Sonora, California

Sonora's reputation grew. Nevills would go on to build an even more luxurious hotel in Jamestown, The Nevills Hotel. This hotel, also called the Jamestown Hotel, later burned to the ground in 1915. Fortunately Nevills did not live to see it. He passed away in 1912, ending one of the most flamboyant personalities of the Mother Lode. The Victoria Hotel, now the Sonora Days Inn, remains a lasting reminder of the man who helped shape a small town of the 1890s into a thriving and bustling community.

The first time I visited the Sonora Inn was in the late 1950s. My parents had moved to the area and the Sonora Inn was the *only* place in town to stay.

Later, when I moved to Sonora, I learned more about the history of the hotel. There is an underground tunnel which was built during the Gold Rush so that thieves could not abscond with Mother Lode gold when businessmen went to the bank. During Prohibition, the tunnel, it was rumored, was widely used.

With the arrival of the film industry, movie stars abounded in Sonora, staying, of course, at the only first rate hotel in town: The Sonora Inn. Silent film stars such as William S. Hart and Tom Mix stayed at the Inn and were often feted with fabulous dinners. Over 400 films have been shot in Sonora, and many of the legendary celebrities used the hotel as a place to stay.

With the coming of television, most of the cast and crew of *Little House on the Prairie*, *Bonanza* and dozens of other dramas, have dined at the Inn and were often spotted walking leisurely down the streets of Sonora.

Today, the historic hotel has a total of thirty-four rooms and a more modern motel annex which contains another thirty-four rooms. There are four suites supported by a 110 year-old elevator, one of the oldest in California. A colonnade in the front faces Washington Street and there is also a balcony in back facing the pool. The hotel has a banquet room in the back which seats up to eighty people and a cafe, also facing Washington Street.

For more information on Sonora Days Inn call: (209) 532-7468 or Toll Free: (866) 732-4010; Fax: (209) 532-4542
E-mail: info@sonoradaysinn.com
Web page: www.sonoradaysinn.com

Location: The Sonora Days Inn is located at the corner of Stockton Road and Washington Street in downtown Sonora.
Mail: 160 S. Washington Street, Sonora, CA 95370

How to get there:

From Fresno: Take Highway 99 north to Merced. Then take Highway J59 north through Snelling to Highway 108, then turn east. Take Highway 49 off ramp to downtown Sonora.

From Sacramento/Stockton: Take Highway 99 south to Manteca. Take Highway 108/120 east through Escalon and Oakdale. Take Highway 49 off ramp to downtown Sonora.

Favorite Recipes from Camacho's Taqueria

Potato Poblano Soup

Ingredients:

> 4 Large Potatoes, peeled and quartered
> 2 Yellow Onions, sliced
> 1 Tbsp. Vegetable Oil
> 4 Poblano Chilies, roasted and peeled
> 2 quarts Chicken Stock
> 1/4 lb. Cheddar Cheese, grated

Method:

Sweat the onions in a large pan with 1 Tbsp. oil. When onions are cooked add the potatoes, Poblanos and chicken stock. Cook until the potatoes are soft. Remove from heat and add the cheese. Let it sit for 20 minutes, then purée and season with salt and pepper and serve.

Calabacitas

Ingredients:

> 2 cups Zucchini, sliced
> 1 Sliced Yellow Onion
> 1 can Creamed Corn
> 1/2 cup Green Chilies, diced
> 1/4 cup Tomatoes, diced
> 1/4 cup Green Onions
> 1/2 cup Jack Cheese

Method:

Sauté the Zucchini and onions for 4 minutes. Then add creamed corn, diced green chili, and tomatoes. When mixture is hot, add green onions, salt and pepper to taste. Melt the cheese on top and serve.

Note: Many restaurants have come and gone at the Sonora Inn. Recently, I sat down with Dave Camacho, the chef of Camacho's Taqueria, inside Sonora Days Inn. He is not, he told me, a professional cook. That is, he was not trained in a cooking school. He just loves good food. For him it is therapy—a break from the more analytical work he has done in the past. What he wants to bring to his restaurant is the food his own family grew up eating—comfort food, what your grandmother once served. Only the finest ingredients are used—all meat is premium cut, only tri-tip, Diestel Turkey and boneless pork.

As of the printing of this book, this restaurant has changed ownership, and is now reopened as Christopher's Ristorante Italiano.

The Gunn House, Sonora, California

The Gunn House 1850
SONORA

No other hotel in Sonora quite defines the Gold Rush era as does The Gunn House. While it did not begin its life as a hotel, it is, nevertheless, a living re-enactment of the story of the men, women and events that transpired when the hope of finding El Dorado drew the world to California. It has gone through many re-incarnations—from a private home in 1850, to a newspaper office, a recorder's office, a hospital, a boarding house, an Italian restaurant and finally, a hotel. The fact that it has survived numerous additions and restorations speaks highly of the current owners who have lovingly carried this architectural gem safely into the 21st century.

Today, traffic slows to a crawl and heads turn when they pass the magnificent brown building on South Washington

Street. One can only breathe a huge sigh of relief that this rare 19th jewel remains in pristine condition—still telling its story—still revealing its secrets to curious modern day explorers.

When Lewis Carstairs Gunn left Philadelphia in 1849, he had attended Columbia University and later Princeton with the goal of entering the ministry. The news of the California gold strike diverted these plans and drew young Lewis, along with thousands of other hopefuls, to the gold fields. Choosing one of the least traveled routes, he made the hazardous journey from New Orleans overland to Mexico, then to the coast of Mazatlan, sailing into San Francisco in August 1849. By the time his ship docked in the city by the bay, hundreds of vessels had already unloaded their anxious argonauts who proceeded to descend upon the mountain streams and valleys of the Sierra Nevada. From Mariposa in the south to Grass Valley in the north, their delirium was driven by the hope of striking it rich.

Lewis Gunn was a man of rare good sense, intelligence and faith. For awhile the prim and proper Philadelphian tried his luck in the diggings near Jamestown. He soon came to realize, however, that the rough and tumble life of a miner was not exactly what he was cut out to do. And, the community certainly needed more than miners. His brother was a doctor and Lewis was somewhat familiar with basic medical remedies. As he handed out advice and suggestions for curing the multiple illnesses that beset the miners, his reputation grew. Doctors were rare in the gold fields, and his services were needed. From pulling teeth to lancing abscesses, to prescribing medicine, Dr. Gunn, as he was now known, was doing better financially as a physician than as a miner.

Dr. Gunn was also a man of letters and on November 10, 1850, he bought a half interest in the *Sonora Herald*. He built a small adobe structure which housed the first newspaper published in the southern mines, becoming its editor and publisher. Miners in the gold fields were isolated from their families back home and news was eagerly sought to re-connect them to loved ones.

By this time, Lewis was feeling this separation from his own family. He missed Elizabeth and his four children acutely. He was afraid he would lose seeing them through their early years. He had been in Sonora almost two years and he felt the paper was established well enough that he could send for his family. He wrote Elizabeth telling her to come west.

In August 1851, Elizabeth, Douglas, Chester, Sarah and Lizzie arrived safely in San Francisco. The family was together at last and celebrations were in order. The Christmas of '51 was not elaborate, but it was certainly joyful. There was a tree, lots of singing, plenty of home-baked goods and hot cider passed around to one and all.

The Gunns lived on the second floor of the small home and office nestled among towering pine and oak trees —the first two-story building in Sonora. They were crowded and Elizabeth complained about the constant dust from outside and the noise of the newspaper downstairs. But they were together. On many a night, the entire family looked up at the night sky, marveling at the brightest stars they had ever seen.

After ten years in Sonora the Gunns decided to move to San Francisco. Educational opportunities for the children were better, and a larger city probably appealed more to Elizabeth. Eventually the family retired in San Diego.

After their departure, the house was used as the county hospital. Later it operated as a boarding establishment—the White House, home to Italian immigrant and grocer J.B. Brescia. From 1913 to 1955, the building at 286 South Washington was known as the Rosa Italia Hotel or more popularly as Mama Bisordi's Italian Restaurant. People far and wide came to feast on Mama's home-cooked meals and hospitality. Additions to the establishment were made accommodating a large dining room which seated more than forty people offering family type dinners—all you could eat for prices that would be the culinary envy of every Sonoran today.

In the early 1960s, The Gunn House was purchased by Margaret Dienelt and underwent a huge restoration. For the first time it became a hotel with eighteen rooms. All the rooms were furnished with antiques and the hotel took on the appearance it has today. In 2002 the hotel was purchased by the current owners, Mike and Shirley Sarno.

When I visited recently, I asked about the small adobe structure which originally housed the Gunn family and newspaper. It is, I am told, still intact, incorporated into the later structural additions. I strolled to the back of the hotel, past a Koi pond, through a large commodious area where one can converse with guests, or simply hang out, to a bar with a welcoming fireplace for those long winter evenings and still further on, a large hillside pool for summer fun. Each room is beautifully furnished with private bath, and there are no phones to break the spell of the quiet ambiance still enjoyed by guests.

If the Gunn family were to return today, they would be surprised that the old family homestead is still there. They would no doubt be taken aback at the grandiose hotel which surrounds their small adobe home, but they would be pleased that The Gunn House represents to tourists and locals alike the incredible historic frenzy of the 1849 gold rush. The community they helped build is known throughout the world, and visitors who walk the same historic steps that the Gunns once trod still find the same welcome mat waiting.

For more information on The Gunn House call: (209) 532-3421

Innkeepers are Mike and Shirley Sarno

E-mail: info@gunnhousehotel.com

Web page: www.gunnhousehotel.com

Location: 286 S. Washington Street in downtown Sonora.

Mail: 286 S. Washington Street, Sonora, CA 95370

How to get there:

From Fresno...

Take Highway 99 north to Merced. Then take Highway J59 north through Snelling to Highway 108, turn east. Take Highway 49 off ramp to downtown Sonora.

From Sacramento and Stockton...

Take Highway 99 south to Manteca. Take Highway 108/120 east through Escalon and Oakdale. Take Highway 49 off ramp to downtown Sonora.

Since there is no longer a restaurant on the premises, I found an old recipe from an 1861 Christmas past which comes from historian Sharon Marovich. See *Chispa*, "Memories of Christmas Past." Vol. 24, No. 2, Oct-Dec. 1984.

Recipes from Christmas 1861

Old Fashioned Plum Pudding

Ingredients:

3 cups Suet
1 Pkg. Raisins
1 Pkg. Currants
1 cup Chopped Walnuts
5 cups Flour
1 cup Bread Crumbs
8 Beaten Eggs
1 1/2 cups Sugar
1/2 tsp. Baking Powder
1 tsp. Vanilla
Pinch of salt

NOTE: If you're making a traditional steamed pudding, especially a plum pudding, there is no substitute for suet.

Suet is the hard fat from around the kidneys of cows and sheep. Do not confuse it with fat from other parts of the animal that may be sold as suet but does not have the same properties. Most of the suet sold in supermarkets is of indeterminate quality and age, and quite likely intended for bird feeders.

A butcher would be a reliable source for suet.

Method:

Mix all ingredients together. Put in a clean cloth and tie at the top. Put in boiling water to cover pudding and boil for five hours. Do not burn. Serve warm with Lemon Sauce, below...

Lemon Sauce

1 cup Sugar
1 Tbsp. Cornstarch
1 Tbsp. Butter
1 cup boiling water.
Vanilla or Lemon Extract to taste.

Combine sugar, cornstarch and boiling water. Cool slowly until thickened and clear, stirring constantly. Remove from heat and add vanilla or lemon extract to taste. And butter.

*This recipe was attributed to Cornish ancestors of the
Nicholls family of Soulsbyville.*

The Fallon Hotel in winter

Photo by Carol Giordano

Fallon (House) Hotel 1857
COLUMBIA

*W*hen most people think of the Fallon House, they think of a theater and the old fashioned Ice Cream Parlor. For some reason the fact that there is also a hotel next to both the theater and parlor is often overlooked. One of the reasons is that the hotel closed in 1947 and was not re-opened until 1986. This was following a two-year renovation. And what a renovation.

The Fallon House Hotel and City Hotel in Columbia are

run by a privately-owned company. While many of the privately-owned hotels mentioned in *Oysters on the Half Shell* have been lovingly and painstakingly restored by their owners, the State Park system demands an entirely different set of codes and standards. And they are tough. For starters, all the restoration that takes part in Columbia State Historic Park must follow the Federal Secretary of the Interior's restoration guidelines for historic properties. They must also follow the California Historical Building Code and they must conform to the California Environmental Quality Act. On top of this, they have to follow two Public Resource code sections. These codes are complex and time consuming. Adding her input to all of this was Dr. Linda Bissonnette who is Columbia State Historic Park District's cultural specialist.

When I spoke with Linda regarding the Fallon House she explained the process the structures within the park had to go through in order to be restored. First, an historian must research the buildings, investigating archives, interviewing residents, exploring any documentation to see what changes have to be made in order to bring the structure back to an authentic appearance. The building must be restored with the goal of duplicating it as close to the original as possible. Also, another overriding factor is that whatever is done, the public must be taken into account to make sure the building is as safe as possible. For example, it must be seismically retrofitted.

Columbia's population at the height of the Gold Rush was about 16,000. Then, the Comstock Lode was discovered in 1859, luring miners away. In the 1860s there were severe storms, followed by severe droughts. Between 1870 and 1900, the population declined further and the number of people dropped to less than 1000. In spite of this, the residents who remained were devoted to keeping the community as authentic as possible. They were aware of Columbia's history and its importance and tended to work as a group striving to keep their own and new structures as truthful to the history of the community as possible. In some cases, homes from elsewhere were moved onto the property to enhance the historic ambiance.

When I explained what my book was about, Linda added some interesting facts about the food of those who had once lived in Columbia. Apparently the miners' diets consisted of what they called "high" and "low." In other words, when digging in the mines they ate low, but on weekends when they hit town, they ate high: oysters, peaches and champagne! Early menus were English in style, hence boiled meats were eaten. Later, as more men arrived and prosperity grew, French items appeared on menus. Looking over those early menus, today's patrons might be surprised to learn that lobster, artichokes, mushrooms, crepes and truffles were on the bill of fare, imported from France, China, the Pacific Northwest and Mexico. Judging from the Hoff Store archeological site, it was found that a great deal of pork made up much of what people ate. In addition there was Lobscouse, Skillygalee and Dandy Funk, dishes that have long since passed from sight. Lobscouse was a hash or stew made from vegetables, packed-meat, and hardtack. Skillygalee was made by soaking hardtack in water and then frying it in lard. For dessert, Dandy Funk was prepared by baking crumbled hardtack with fat, molasses and cinnamon or raisins. The miners did suffer from stomach ills and used a lot of pepper sauce, pickles and bitters which, Linda said, they drank straight! Keep in mind, she told me, items were shipped in from all over the world, so there was a lot of variety.

After this introduction to the park, it was a treat for me when Charlotte Rovera from the City Hotel in Columbia showed me through the Fallon House. Frankly, what I saw came as a total surprise. The wallpapers were the most gorgeous I had ever seen. When I asked Charlotte about them, I learned they came from a firm in Benecia, Bradbury and Bradbury, a nationally known restoration company. Some of the papers were reproduced using a silk screen process. It is absolutely a first class job.

I asked Charlotte who was responsible for the interior design. She told me Pauline Grenbeaux Spear of Sacramento. Ms. Spear left no stone unturned in restoring the old hotel to

104

its former grandeur. She reviewed state documents and conducted personal interviews to make sure the restoration was as accurate as could be. Her other restorations included the State Capitol and the imposing Stanford Mansion. The Fallon House was in the hands of a master.

As I strolled through the rooms I could not keep up with Charlotte. I kept pausing and staring back at the high walls and ceilings glistening with gold and silver. Some of the original furniture of the 1870s was retrieved as well as pieces collected from all over Columbia and the state collections. What a treasure. When guests arrive, they can be certain that nothing in the hotel dates from after 1900 with one exception—the bathrooms. One of the highlights in the parlor is a Turkish Conversation Chair, where couples can get a little closer to each other without drawing attention to themselves.

The Fallon Hotel, as it is now called, has fifteen rooms, however fourteen are open to the public. The extra room is used by the custodian. There are petite rooms and larger rooms and one large master suite with views from the balcony. All the rooms are irresistibly furnished with period antiques. And, of course, there is a resident ghost. He is friendly.

Originally, the Fallon House was known as the Maine House, built in the early 1850s when Columbia was packed with miners and the entire spectrum of gold seekers. Later, Mr. Owen Fallon, a hard rock miner, took it over after a fire razed Columbia in 1857. This was followed by yet another fire two years later. Finally Mr. Fallon constructed a brick building. In 1863 he purchased the adjoining buildings and, in 1864, the entire complex was known as the Fallon House. Later Fallon's son, James, took over the running of the hotel. He built a new theater and dance hall behind the hotel in 1885. Four years later in 1889, Thomas Conlin purchased the Fallon House, remodeling and adding the arched doorway in the center of the building—using marble from the local Columbia quarry.

For the next fifty years, the area languished. Then in 1922 the artist, Otheto Weston, discovered the town of Columbia. Spellbound, she loved the community so much, that in 1930

105

The Fallon Hotel in summer

she opened Otheto's Studio on Main Street. From her sketches and oils, she painted everything in and around Columbia, immortalizing the town forever in her book, *Mother Lode Album*. She discovered a group in San Francisco called "Save the Landmarks League." Hoping they might be able to help, she wrote them and included her sketches. It was not easy, but her paintings and photography introduced Columbia to a wider audience. She launched a drive to save the buildings. Because of her efforts a group of concerned citizens formed the Historic Mining Towns' Preservation League to preserve, not only Columbia, but also other historic mining towns. Otheto continued to press for some kind of recognition of Columbia so that its special character could be preserved for others.

As early as the 1920s, however, plans were underway to restore some of California's special areas. The California Legislature commissioned Frederick Law Olmsted, Jr. to travel

106

through California looking for places to form a State Park. In the '40s, Dr. and Mrs. James McConnell picked up the gauntlet and their work resulted in Governor Earl Warren's establishment on July 15, 1945, of Columbia State Historic Park.

———————————◆———————————

For more about the Fallon Hotel and Fallon House Theatre call: (209) 532-1470

Location: 11175 Washington St., Columbia, California 95310

How to get there:

From Fresno: Take Highway 99 north to Merced. Then take Highway J59 north through Snelling to Highway 108, turn east. Take Highway 49 off ramp to downtown Sonora. From Sonora, Columbia is five miles north on Highway 49 to Parrotts Ferry Road. Take Parrotts Ferry Road into Columbia State Historic Park.

From Sacramento/Stockton: Take Highway 99 south to Manteca. Take Highway 108/120 east through Escalon and Oakdale. Take Highway 49 off ramp to downtown Sonora. From Sonora, Columbia is five miles north on Highway 49 to Parrotts Ferry Road. Take Parrotts Ferry Road into Columbia State Historic Park.

Pasties are a classic recipe from Cornish Coal Miners which found its way into Columbia. My reason for including this is one of sentiment. When my husband I flew into Columbia, we headed for a favorite place which served Pasties. Today it houses the offices of Central Valley District Headquarters for the park.

We were told that Pasties originated in Cornwall, England, but generally Pasties were packed into lunches of Cornish coal miners.

Cornish Pasty

These are meat pies— basically a beef stew sealed in a pastry shell. We loved them!

Ingredients:

Pasty Crust:
> 4 Cups flour
> 1 Tbsp. Sugar
> 1/2 tsp. Salt.
> 1 3/4 cups of butter (or lard)

Use a pastry blender to cut in the butter (lard) until it resembles coarse crumbs. Separately mix together...

> 1 Egg
> 1/2 cup Ice Water
> 1 Tbsp. White Vinegar

Add this slowly to the flour, sugar, salt and butter. Let rest for 1/2 an hour. Turn onto a floured work surface, divide dough into 6 portions and roll each one out into a circle about 1/4" thick.

Pasty Filling:
> 2 lbs. Round Steak or Boneless Rump Roast, cut in cubes
> 2 or 3 Medium Size Potatoes, peeled and chopped
> 1 Turnip or Rutabaga, finely chopped
> 1 Small Onion, chopped
> 1 1/2 tsp. Salt
> 1/4 tsp. Pepper
> 1 tsp. Worcestershire Sauce (a modern addition)

Method:

Heat oven to 400°. Mix filling ingredients and place a portion onto a pastry circle at one end. Moisten dough edges, fold over top half and pinch the dough to seal it. Cut slits in the top of the dough as heat vents. Bake until golden brown, about 45-50 min.

"*People, when they first
come to America,
whether as travelers or settlers,
become aware of a
new and agreeable feeling:
that the whole country
is their oyster.*"

Journalist, Alistair Cooke
1908-2004

The City Hotel in Columbia, California

The City Hotel 1856
COLUMBIA

The City Hotel is right in the heart of Columbia State Historic Park. The town's origin, like that of other Gold Rush communities began just two years after John Marshall's historic discovery of gold in Coloma, California in 1848. Would-be prospectors swarmed throughout the entire length of the Sierra's famous gold belt. Eventually miners discovered Wood's Creek in today's Jamestown, then began searching for

111

other locations, hoping to find the precious yellow metal. Invariably they discovered Columbia. In 1849 Dr. Thaddeus Hildreth and his younger brother, George, followed an old Indian trail that led into Columbia Gulch. Gold was discovered there in March 1850 and the rush was on. In an area of just 640 acres, more gold was eventually found there than in any other area of equal size in the Western Hemisphere.

At first the town was called Hildreth's Diggings after Dr. Thaddeus Hildreth, but was later changed to Columbia. There were three dozen bars or more, gambling, dance halls, prostitutes, two theaters, seventeen dry goods and produce stores, four hotels, half a dozen boarding houses, two barber shops, three drug stores, laundries, carpenter shops, tobacconists, wagon makers, blacksmiths, doctors, lawyers, printing shops, a brewery and of course, Chinatown. Miners in Columbia would extract more than fifty-five million dollars in gold. With this bonanza came stories—lots of them. As it was told, one lone miner found a twenty-nine pound gold nugget in 1857! And, Columbia would, some insist, miss becoming the capital of California in 1853 by a small margin. Today she is known as the Gem of the Southern Mines.

The City Hotel began humbly enough. The great fire of 1854 raced through Columbia destroying the small timber-framed building which stood on the spot where today's City Hotel is located. But within days, many new brick buildings were under construction.

A young man, George Morgan, had arrived from England and he acquired the property. He opened a six-room hotel known as the Welcome Inn. His building was burned just one month later, not unusual in the Gold Rush era.

In April 1856, Morgan began the construction of a two-story brick building. It was small, just 25x54, and housed a billiard saloon and ale house—necessary establishments when the population of the town was overwhelmingly male. The men worked all day and looked forward to relieving the boredom and enjoying a little entertainment in the evening.

In 1856 a newspaper, The *Columbia Gazette,* occupied the upper story of Morgan's establishment. Then again, another fire raced through town in 1857 causing a loss of $5,000. Morgan did not hesitate. This time his plans were more grandiose. He built a much larger establishment called The What Cheer House. In 1861 the Columbia Opera Company performed in Morgan's hotel. Another fire in 1866 destroyed the building and again it was restored and reopened and continued to be operated from this point on as a hotel and saloon.

By the 1870s, most of the miners had left Columbia. The Gold Rush was over. The few people who remained made the transition from gold mining to farming. In 1874 the name of the hotel was changed to Morgan's City Hotel. It contained twenty rooms, a bar-room, dining rooms and a sitting room, taking on some of the character it has today. For reasons that are not clear Morgan took his own life in 1891.

The hotel remained in the Morgan family, however, until 1911 when, after another fire, it passed to the Dante Cinelli family. Dante's wife, Mary, took charge, refurbishing and restoring it. During this time the large two-story frame addition was rebuilt which contained a large kitchen and several more lodging rooms.

It was during this time that The City Hotel's reputation grew throughout California. Transitioning from stagecoach to automobiles, the somewhat remote pristine Sierra towns were now more accessible to everyone. Tourists came from all over the world. Film scouts from Hollywood began searching out more rural locations for their silent Western films. A tradition was born and film stars such as Mary Pickford and Tom Mix fell in love with the area.

With the Great Depression in the 1930s travel slowed and the central Sierra did not see the number of visitors it had once enjoyed. The City Hotel closed its doors in the 1940s— only the bar remained open. For the next twenty years, Columbia's streets became vacant and only a few old timers hung around.

Although the town's restoration began in 1947, it wasn't until 1974 that The City Hotel building was restored and reopened. The hotel's journey had come full circle from 1854 to 1974, and continues today into the 21st century.

In addition to all of this history, there are many old

113

fashioned events held in Columbia. In April, "Last Night on the Titanic Dinner Show" is held. The City Hotel takes you back to that memorable voyage through stories, music, food, and wines. "Cousin Jack Weekend" in June celebrates the skills of the Cornishmen who tapped the wealth of Mother Lode gold. There is "Speakeasy Night" in July, which tells about the special year 1928 when hope for the repeal of prohibition ran high. Bootleggers, mobsters and G-Men all found their way to The City Hotel to get a little "something extra" in their tea. And there is the "Gold Baron's Ball" in October. Guests feast on a Champagne supper, dance, and hear stories of Spanish nobility. In October there is the "Black Bart Dinner." The notorious highwayman's zesty life is retold with staged shootings and hangings to boot, all of it accompanied by a leisurely dinner at the hotel. In December the famous "Victorian Christmas Feast" delights children and adults alike.

What began in 1922, when one artist fell in love with Columbia, to today's Columbia State Historic Park which has hosted tourists from all over the world seems like a fairy tale story. Many of these people come not just to see Columbia, but to research their family history. Perhaps a relative "way back when" came to California in 1849, and their descendants are trying to trace them for their family trees.

There are also endless stories about the more than 300 films shot in and around the town of Columbia, including *High Noon* with Gary Cooper and Grace Kelly.

For more information call Columbia State Historic Park: (209) 588-9128. Columbia State Historic Park also houses research archives and a collection which can be reached at (209) 536-2888.

Reservations: The City Hotel: (209) 532-1479 or through their **Website**: www.cityhotel.com

E-Mail: info@cityhotel.com

Location: Columbia State Historic Park, Main Street, Columbia, Calif.

How to get there:

From Fresno...

Take Highway 99 north to Merced. Then take Highway J59 north through Snelling to Highway 108, turn east. Take Highway 49 off ramp to downtown Sonora. From Sonora, Columbia is five miles north on Highway 49. Take Parrotts Ferry Road into Columbia State Historic Park.

From Sacramento and Stockton...

Take Highway 99 south to Manteca. Take Highway 108/120 east through Escalon and Oakdale. Take Highway 49 off ramp to downtown Sonora. From Sonora, Columbia is five miles north on Highway 49. Take Parrotts Ferry Road into Columbia State Historic Park.

Recipes from The City Hotel

Butterhead Lettuce Wedge
with Smoked Tomato Relish & Asparagus Vinaigrette
Serves 4

Ingredients:

> 1 Head Butter Lettuce
> 1/2 lb. Boursin Cheese
> 1 Bunch Fresh Asparagus, cut into pieces (see below)
> 2 Tbls. Red Wine Vinegar
> 1/2 cup Olive Oil
> 12 each Yellow and Red Pear and Grape Tomatoes
> 1 Medium Red Onion, julienne
> 1 Green Pepper, sliced
> 1 Tbls. Extra Virgin Olive Oil
> Salt and Pepper
> French Bread, cut into 1/4" thick slices

Method Asparagus Vinaigrette:

Cut green part of asparagus all the way to the stalk into 1/8" slices. Boil asparagus until very soft. Drain off water and purée in food processor. Strain pulp through a medium coarse colander. Discard pulp left in colander. Let purée cool. After asparagus purée is cool, add red wine vinegar and whisk rapidly while pouring in 1/2 cup olive oil. Salt and pepper to taste.

Method Smoked Tomato Relish:

In backyard smoker or on a grill, smoke tomatoes for about 15 minutes (not too soft). After smoked, cut tomatoes lengthwise in half. Toss in a bowl with red onion and green pepper. Sprinkle salt over mixture and toss again with 1 Tbsp. extra virgin olive oil.

116

Method:

1. Create oval croutons by slicing French Bread into 1/4" thick slices, brushing with extra virgin olive oil and baking in an oven until golden brown. After croutons are cool, spread 2 oz. of Boursin Cheese to cover top of the crouton.
2. Place 1/4 wedge of lettuce on plate. Garnish with Smoked Tomato Relish and drizzle with Asparagus Vinaigrette. Serve with a Boursin crouton.

Lobster and Gruyere Torte
Serves 4

Ingredients:

6 oz. Lobster Tail
4 Large Shallots, caramelized (see below)
1/2 cup Gruyere Cheese, shredded
2 Eggs
1 lb. Softened Cream Cheese
2 Leaves Chiffonade* Fresh Basil
Salt and Pepper
2 cups coarse Bread Crumbs
3/4 cup Butter, melted
1 tsp. Cracked Black Pepper

*Chiffonade: cut into thin, fine ribbons

Method:

Julienne four large shallots. Place in small saucepan with butter over medium heat. Slowly sauté until brown and fully caramelized. Set aside to cool. Dice raw lobster tail into 1/4" pieces. Mix together softened cream cheese and eggs until fully blended. Fold in lobster and basil (approximately 1/2 tsp. salt and 1/4 tsp. pepper). Add shallots and half of the Gruyere cheese.

In a separate bowl, create crust by adding the butter slowly to the bread crumbs and pepper until a dough-like consistency is formed. Line the bottom and sides of a 9" pie tin with the bread crumbs. Pour in cheese mixture (above). Sprinkle remaining Gruyere Cheese on top and bake in 350° oven until center is set (approximately 40 minutes). Allow to chill before cutting. Reheat individual slices to serve.

Roasted Red Pepper Cream

Ingredients:

1/2 cup Fennel Bulb, julienne
2 each Red Bell Peppers, roasted, peeled
1 cup Heavy Cream
2 Shallots, chopped
1 Tbsp. Olive Oil
Salt and Pepper

Method:

Preheat oven 375° F
1. Roast two red bell peppers by rubbing outside of pepper with olive oil. Place on a sheet pan in 375° F oven until skin darkens and looks scorched. Remove from oven and while hot, place in plastic bag to steam. Seal or tie end of bag.
2. After peppers are cool, the skin will peel off. Discard seeds, skin and stems. Rough cut the red pepper into chunks. Over medium heat, sauté red pepper, fennel and shallots in 1 Tbsp. olive oil. Cook until fennel is soft and tender. Add heavy cream and simmer until sauce is reduced by half.
3. Place in food processor and purée. Add salt and pepper to taste.
Serve warm over torte.

Bone-In Ribeye Wrapped In Pancetta
with Pearl Onion Pan Sauce and Stilton Butter

Ingredients:

One 12 oz. Bone-in Ribeye Steak
3 oz. Slice Pancetta*
1 cup Beef Stock
6 each Pearl Onions
1/4 cup Red Wine

*Pancetta is an Italian Bacon that is cured with salt, pepper, and other spices, but is not smoked.

Continued

118

Salt and Pepper to taste
1 Tbsp. Olive Oil

Stilton Butter

1/2 cup Stilton Cheese, room temperature
2 Tbls. whole butter, room temperature

Method:

1. Warm cheese and butter to room temperature. Mix together in a bowl with a rubber spatula until well blended.

2. Place in a cigar shape on waxed paper or plastic wrap. Roll into a 1" diameter link. Place in freezer to harden.

3. After mixture has set up cut into 1/2" slices. Place on ribeye steak at service.

Method for Rib Eye:

1. Clean bone of ribeye and wrap in aluminum foil. Wrap meat of ribeye with Pancetta and tie with kitchen twine to hold in place. Salt and pepper both sides of ribeye.

2. Brown in sauté pan with 1 Tbsp. olive oil over high heat. Brown both sides.

3. Place pan in 350° oven and cook to medium rare (120° F internal temperature) and remove from oven.

4. Take ribeye from pan. While pan is still hot, place pearl onions in drippings over medium heat and brown on all sides. Pour in red wine to retrieve drippings (deglaze) from pan. Add beef stock and boil until reduced by half. Salt and pepper to taste.

Rabbit and Truffle Ballotine

Ingredients:

> 1 lb. Rabbit Meat, ground
> 1 Egg, beaten
> 1/4 cup Heavy Cream
> 6 Strips Bacon
> 1/4 cup Brandy or Cognac
> 1 Tbsp. Chopped Truffle Pieces
> 3/4 tsp.Salt
> 3/4 tsp. Pepper
> 1/4 tsp. Nutmeg
> 1/4 tsp. Fresh Thyme Leaves

Method:

Debone a rabbit like you would a chicken and grind meat in a grinder or food processor. Mix all ingredients except the bacon with the meat, making sure there is a consistent texture. Line a small (4 cup) loaf pan with 4 strips of bacon. Fill the lined pan with the meat mixture. Place two strips of bacon on top. Butter a piece of aluminum foil and place on top of bacon to seal. Place a clean dish towel in a 13"x11" roasting pan. Fill the pan halfway with water and place loaf pan in water bath. Place in 325° F. oven and cook until center reads 160° F on meat thermometer (about 1 1/2 hours), Remove from oven and let rest for 15-20 minutes. Turn loaf pan over on cutting board to remove ballotine. Discard bacon. Slice ballotine into 1/2" slices with a sharp knife. Serve next to ribeye with sauce.

Pistachio Baklava
with Grilled Pineapple and Chocolate Sauce
Yield about 30 squares

Grilled Golden Pineapple

Ingredients:

1 Fresh Whole Golden Pineapple
1 Slice Plain Cheesecake (approximately 1 1/2 cups)
2 1/2 Cups Vanilla Ice Cream

Method:

Peel and core pineapple, leaving the fruit whole so it can be cut into 1 inch rings. Grill rings over hot grill to mark the pineapple and soften it. Set aside.

Mix cheesecake (most bakeries and deli selections will sell individual slices of cheesecake) and softened ice cream with beaters until thoroughly mixed together. Return ice cream mixture immediately to freezer to refreeze.

Continue...

Pistachio Baklava

Ingredients:

Stack flat on work surface:
1 lb. Phyllo Dough

Finely chop or coarsely grind:
3 cups Pistachios, toasted

Stir together in small bowl:
1/4 cup Sugar
1 tsp. Grated Lemon Zest
1/2 tsp. Ground Cinnamon

Melt:
1/2 lb. Unsalted Butter (2 sticks)

Continue...

121

Method for the Baklava:

Trim Phyllo dough into 13"x 9" sheets, saving scraps for later use. Cover the stack with plastic wrap and a damp towel. Place 2 Phyllo sheets in baking pan and brush top sheet evenly with melted butter. Add 2 more sheets and brush with butter, repeat once more for a total of 6 sheets. Sprinkle with half the pistachios, then half of the sugar mixture. Cover filling with 2 Phyllo sheets, butter the top sheet and repeat until there are 6 sheets on top of the filling. Cover with remaining nuts and sugar mixture. Cover with all remaining Phyllo sheets, adding them 2 at a time, buttering only the second sheet each time. Brush the top with remaining butter. Using sharp serrated knife so that the pastry will not be crushed, cut through all layers to make 2" diamonds or squares. This is important because you will not be able to cut the Baklava once it is baked without crushing the pastry. It also allows the syrup to soak in and around each piece. Bake for 30 minutes. Reduce temperature to 300° F. Continue to bake until Baklava is golden brown (45 to 60 minutes).

During the last 30 minutes of baking, combine following in a sauce pan:

> 1 1/3 cups Sugar
> 1 1/3 cups Water
> 1/3 cup Honey
> 1 Tbsp. Fresh Lemon Juice
> Zest of 1 Orange, cut in large strips.

Method:

Bring mixture to gentle boil, reduce heat and simmer uncovered for 15 minutes. Strain hot syrup and pour evenly over baked Baklava. Let cool completely, at least 4 hours, at room temperature before serving.

Continue...

Chocolate Sauce

Ingredients:

1/2 cup Light Cream or...
    (1/4 cup Heavy Cream and 1/4 cup whole milk).
1 to 2 Tbsp. Sugar
1 Tbsp. Unsalted Butter
4 oz. Semisweet or Bittersweet Chocolate, finely chopped
1 tsp. Vanilla (or 1 Tbsp. Dark Rum or Cognac)

Method:

Grind chocolate to crumbs in food processor. Then in a saucepan, bring cream, sugar and butter, stirring constantly, to a rolling boil in saucepan. Remove pan from heat and immediately add chocolate that has been ground into crumbs in food processor. Let stand one minute, then whisk until smooth. Whisk in vanilla (or rum or cognac).

Sauce can be prepared entirely in food processor. With motor running, add simmering cream mixture. By the time the last of the cream has gone in, sauce will be melted and smooth.

Sauce can be covered and refrigerated up to 2 weeks.

Reheat over low heat, whisking in (off heat) a little hot water if sauce looks oily. Serve warm or cold; thin a cold sauce with water as needed.

To serve, place Pineapple Ring on plate and top with a scoop of ice cream. Side with a slice of Pistachio Baklava.
Top Ice Cream with Chocolate Sauce.

Murphys Hotel painted by Margaret Roberts

The Murphys Historic Hotel & Lodge 1856

MURPHYS

*W*hen the first sounds of "Eureka!" ricocheted throughout the Mother Lode in 1848-49, gold seekers came to the Central Sierra from almost every corner of the globe. One of the towns they settled was Murphys —begun when a group of men known as the Murphy Party arrived. By 1851, however, the town took on a new name, Murphy's New Diggins. This eventually was changed to Murphy's Camp, popularly named after the Murphy brothers and today, it's simply called Murphys.

124

Unlike a lot of other miners, John Murphy was one of those fortunate men who truly struck it rich. He made his claim work well. By 1849 he left Murphys with six mules carrying his gold dust in nothing less than seventeen pouches. Wow! He came early and left early. He must have taken it all with him as well, because Murphys never achieved the reputation as an important gold-bearing town. Unlike Sonora, Columbia, Angels Camp or a dozen other communities spread along the great Mother Lode, Murphys was known more for its quartz than for its gold.

Murphys became famous, in any case, as a stop-over for the Matteson's Stage en route from Milton to Calaveras Big Trees. The beautiful giant sequoias are touted as one of the natural wonders of the world. Mercer Caverns was discovered in 1885 and by that time, Yosemite was beginning to attract people from all over the world. In order to house and entertain visitors, a hotel was built in 1855-56 known originally as the James Sperry and John Perry Hotel.

Unlike the other wooden hotels and establishments built in the 1850s, the owners had the good sense to build a brick structure with iron shutters. In spite of that, the hotel was badly damaged when fire raced through the small community in 1859. By 1861, however, the hotel once again opened its doors.

In 1861 the *Alta California* newspaper ran the following advertisement:

"The hotel kept by Messrs. Sperry and Perry is unsurpassed by any public house outside of San Francisco. The table is supplied, amongst other luxuries, with fresh vegetables from the ranches daily. I must not forget to mention another luxury—the soft water which is conveyed to the hotel from a spring a mile distant. Although it is not required to cool it, the proprietors are supplied with crystal blocks from their snow house at Big Trees."

"MITCHLER'S HOTEL", MURPHYS, CAL. MRS. ELIZABETH MITCHLER & SONS. PROPR'S.

After the Sperrys, the hotel was run by Mrs. Mitchler and became known as Mitchler's Hotel, the Atwood in 1881, and a host of other owners followed. By 1945 the hotel became widely known as the Murphys Hotel.

People come from Australia, China, Japan, Central and South America, Africa, Europe and India to stay at the Murphys. Lords and ladies, princes and princesses dined here. If you look at the hotel register, now at the Calaveras County Historical Society, the following people were guests: President Ulysses S. Grant, writer Thomas Hardy, Charles Boles (Black Bart), Samuel Clemens (Mark Twain), writer Harriet Ward Beecher Stowe, Horatio Alger, Thomas Lipton (tea), Daniel Webster, Susan B. Anthony, members of Napoleon's family, the Count Rothschild, George Hearst, John Jacob Astor, financier J.P. Morgan and a host of others. The hotel rooms bear the names of these famous people.

When I visited the hotel recently, I met owner, Dorian Faught, who is undertaking a huge $1.2 million dollar restoration and addition. He plans to add eighteen duplex cottages, seventy-two new rooms, a 2000 square foot conference room and a pool. In addition he plans to build a large courtyard with upscale shopping and a large restaurant and exhibition kitchen. Dorian even envisions a stage for dinner shows.

I sat down for lunch in a step-down intimate cellar-like dining room with an old oil lamp hanging overhead, historical pictures of Murphys on the original stone walls and proceeded to peruse the chef's menu. There was a Turkey and Cranberry Croissant Sandwich—Cranberry Walnut Relish with lettuce, tomato and Swiss Cheese on a fluffy croissant; Sautéed Crab Cakes lightly seasoned with scallions and bread crumbs with a tartar sauce and fruit salsa; a Veggie Croissant with avocado, sprouts, tomato, red peppers, onions cucumbers and cream cheese. To keep it simple, I ordered fish and chips and was served four large pieces of cod and tons of chips. The price is right and the service is excellent.

After lunch, I strolled around the hotel. There is a magnificent park nearby, a flowing stream year round, a gazebo where band concerts play, the Black Bart Theatre and the town library. And on the day I visited, a horse-drawn carriage passed. For lovers of the Old West, it can all be found in Murphys.

And, of course, the Murphys Hotel has a resident ghost. What old Mother Lode hotel does not have one? It began, the story goes, in 1860, when a young chambermaid fell in love with a gold miner. He went off to seek his fame and fortune while she waited for his return. Eleanor lived the rest of her life waiting for her lover to return. Alas, he never showed up, so apparently, she haunts the hotel instead.

For more information call Murphys Historic Hotel:
(800) 532-7684; (209) 728-3444; Fax (209) 728-1590
Reservations: reservations@murphyshotel.com

E-mail: beth@murphyshistoric.com

Web page: www.murphyshotel.com

Location: 457 Main St., Murphys, CA 95247

How to get there:

From the west, take State Highway 4 east from Angels Camp approximately 12 miles to the town of Murphys, and turn left at the "Main Street."

From Sonora, take Highway 49 north to Parrotts Ferry Road. Turn right and continue through Columbia to Highway 4 (approx. 9 miles). Turn right on Highway 4 (east) to Murphys.

Recipes from the Murphys Hotel

Murphys Historic Hotel Crab Cakes

Portions: 27 (two 2 oz. Crab Cakes each)

Ingredients:

5 lbs. Crab Meat
3 cups Bread Crumbs
5 Eggs
1 Bunch Green Onions, chopped
3/4 cup Dijon Mustard
3/4 cup Mayonnaise
2 tsp. Dry Ginger
Fruit Salsa
5 Lemons, cut into 6 wedges each

128

Method:

1. Drain crab meat well
2. Combine all ingredients
3. Mix. Mixture should have a slightly sticky consistency
4. Form into 2 oz. patties and lightly flour.
5. Cook in hot oil or butter until golden brown on each side.

To serve add a garnish of Fruit Salsa and a Lemon Wedge

Murphys Historic Hotel Lamb Shanks
Prepared by Dorian Faught

Ingredients:

12 Lamb Shanks (approximately 14 oz)
Olive Oil

Breading Flour: (This may look like a lot, but some is for the gravy).
1 1/2 cups Flour
2 Tbsp. Sea Salt
1 Tbsp. coarse Black Pepper
1 Tbsp. White Pepper
2 Tbsp. Granulated Garlic

Gravy Ingredients:
1 Bunch of Celery
3 White Onions
8-10 Carrots
3-4 lbs. Red Potatoes
White Wine
Whole Milk

Method:

Mix Breading Flour ingredients. Using a deep braising pot, slightly moisten lamb shanks with water and roll in breading flour. Braise all sides including the end, until brown.

Continued...

Sautéed Vegetables for Gravy:

In a several separate pans, sauté the diced celery, onions, carrots and potatoes until onions and celery are translucent, turning several times. Sprinkle with sea salt and coarse black pepper. Deglaze each pan of vegetable gravy ingredients with white wine. Set the completed gravy stock off to the side.

Place one layer of lamb shanks in a roasting pan and cover with sautéed vegetable gravy mixture. With the olive oil left over in the braising pan, introduce breading flour a little at a time, adding white wine and whole milk (this will become curdled so you will need to add water to finish gravy to the consistency you want). Constantly whisk until flour has been cooked, scraping pan often. Pour gravy over the top of sautéed vegetables and lamb shanks. Cover with tin foil.

Bake at 350° for 2 1/2 hours or until fork tender.
Mmmmm—sounds good: let's eat.

*"What can be more foolish
than to think that all this rare fabric
of heaven and earth could come
by chance, when all the skill of art
is not able to make an oyster!"*

Writer, Anatole France
(aka Anatole Francois Thibault)
1844-1924

Avery Hotel was the oldest continuously-operated hotel in Calaveras Co.

The Avery Hotel 1851
AVERY

While the old Avery Hotel is currently closed to diners and guests, the Avery is still intact and privately owned. On a recent visit, I noted two historic markers on the property. According to the historic marker placed on the property by E Clampus Vitus, The Avery Hotel was the oldest continuously-operated hotel in Calaveras County. It was built as a family home in 1851 by Joseph and Sarah Goodell of Maine. The Goodells later relocated to Stockton. In 1853 Peter and Nancy Avery, also of Maine, began operating it as a hotel. Famous guests have included Alfalfa of *Our Gang* and such western legends as Black Bart and Roy Rogers. Owners and guests have reliably reported that the benign spirits of a later 19th century sea captain and a locally revered school

Plaque dedicated May 26, 1977

mistress still occasionally visit the hotel. Hazel Fischer, the school mistress, who was responsible for forming the Avery School District, lived in the hotel for thirty years until her death in 1967.

The hotel was purchased in 1922 by the Gotelli family who carried out extensive renovations. Since 1991, further restoration has taken place, but the restaurant and hotel

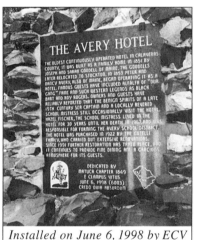

Installed on June 6, 1998 by ECV

are currently closed to guests.

The plaque above, put up by the Native Daughters of the Golden West, reads: "AVERY, formerly Half-Way House Hotel and stagecoach relay station, halfway between Murphys and Big Trees. Settled in the 1850s by Joseph and Sarah Goodell, purchased by Peter Avery, then operated by three generations of Averys... It was used as overnight stops for logging, freight teams and stockmen with herds to and from summer ranges. Later a resort for guests, hunting and fishing parties."

Location: Moran Road, Avery, CA 95224

How to get there:

From Stockton, take Highway 4 heading east to Angels Camp. Stay on Highway 4 east through Murphys to Avery.

Gardner's Hotel in Dorrington in the 1800s

The Dorrington Hotel 1852
DORRINGTON

*O*riginally known as the Cold Springs Ranch or the Gardner Ranch, the Dorrington Hotel is a surprise jewel nestled at 4,800 feet among huge Sugar Pine trees in the Sierra mountains. In the old days it took visitors from dawn to dusk to reach the hotel, transferring from a railroad in Valley Springs to Stockton to the Copperopolis Railroad and finally to a stage line. Today it is minutes from Murphys and Arnold and is well worth the time to see one of the really rare historical gems of the Mother Lode. Fortunately it has had owners who lovingly cared for it from 1852 to the present.

The hotel began life soon after the Gold Rush of 1849. The earliest recorded ownership was that of Benjamin and Clark Stockwell in 1866 or 1868. At that time it was purchased by Rebecca and John Gardner who homesteaded the property in 1880 to obtain clear title. The Gardners built a large house for their growing family and for overnight guests, known as the Gardner's Hotel. The property changed hands again in 1910. Leonard and Florene Anderson owned the hotel from 1948 to 1960 and Arden and Bonnie Saville owned it until 2005.

When I visited the hotel recently, I was met by the Dorrington's new owners, Marc and Dana Lanthier and Jock and Jan Piel. I was warmly greeted and escorted through the hotel. To my surprise, the hotel has three stories, culminating at the top of the stairs with a planned 1,400 square foot family suite currently in the process of restoration. Formerly known as room No. 6, it will have a family room with two murphy beds, a jacuzzi, a large bath with two toilets and a bidet, a kitchen and a large master bedroom which overlooks the beautiful sugar pines. Marc and Jock plan to restore the 1852 redwood beams and make them an integral part of the suite. This uppermost suite will provide ample room for an entire family or couples who want complete privacy.

The other five rooms are beautifully decorated with antique furnishings and all have views of the forest. There is a forty-seat dining room and in the corner, for those stormy nights, there is an authentic 1897 Erie, Pennsylvania, stove. There is, of course, central heat and air conditioning throughout. Outside is a large patio surrounded by pine and English Dutch Elms brought here in 1852.

Marc and Jock are very proud of their spotless commercial kitchen which can serve as many as 200 guests for weddings and banquets. In addition, there are two more 1852 cabins located in the meadow which the owners plan to refurbish.

The chef, Sally Hughes, has been with the hotel for almost ten years, serving up succulent delicacies to her guests and is responsible for bringing the freshest and choicest Italian and Mediterranean delights to the tables.

The Dorrington Hotel and Restaurant

Drawing by Michelle Tsutui

And are there ghosts? Of course. Practically all the hotels in the Mother Lode have stories about out-of-this-world visitors. The Dorrington is no different. It is said that Rebecca Dorrington Gardner has been seen in her blue calico dress and has been heard moving furniture and doors.

Among the hotel's famous visitors was Mark Twain who who carved his initials S.C. (Samuel Clemens) on a tree behind the hotel. Other visitors include western stars Roy Rogers and Dale Evans and motion picture and television star, Robert Stack, who played Elliot Ness in *The Untouchables* and was a former host of *Unsolved Mysteries*.

When I finished my tour, I went next door to the Lube Saloon, dark and moody, with original wooden floors and filled to the rafters with antiques. Its décor hasn't changed in fifty years and that's the way the new owners want to keep it. The food is great.

For more information call The Dorrington Hotel:
(209) 795-5800 for the hotel and (209) 795-1140 for the restaurant.

E-mail: info@dorringtonhotel.com

Web page: www.dorringtonhotel.com

Location: 3431 Highway 4, Dorrington, Calif.

Mail: Dorrington Hotel, P.O. Box 4383, Dorrington, CA. 95223.

How to get there:

From the west, from Highway 99, take State Highway 4 east of Stockton through Angels Camp. Continue east on Highway 4 to the town of Dorrington.

From Sonora, take Highway 49 north to Parrotts Ferry Road. Turn right and continue through Columbia to Highway 4 (approx. 9 miles). Turn right on Highway 4 (east) to Dorrington.

As a tribute to the many Italian immigrants who settled this area during the Gold Rush, we offer these recipes (next 2 pages).

A feeling of nostalgia waves over us as we walk the hillsides near Melones—grapevines still wind their way through the brush and ancient fig trees grace the area—reminiscent of the people who brought a bit of their homeland so long ago to this verdant countryside.

Recipes from The Dorrington Hotel

Caponata (Sicilian Eggplant Relish)
Delicious as a side dish, hot or cold — on bread or alone

Ingredients:

1 Eggplant
1 Medium Onion, cut into 1/2" cubes
1/2 Bunch of Celery, dice into 1/2" cubes
Extra Virgin Olive Oil
1/4 cup Balsamic Vinegar
1/4 cup Sugar
1/4 cup Capers, drain and rinse
1/4 cup Green Olives
1/4 cup Pine Nuts (optional)
2 Tbls. Garlic, chopped
1 small can Tomato Paste.

Method:

1. Cut the eggplant into 1/2 inch cubes, salt pieces, and allow to drain in a colander for 30 minutes. Rinse off salt, and put on a sheet pan with olive oil to coat and bake at 350° F for 20 minutes.

2. Dice celery and onions into 1/2 cubes and sauté in olive oil. Add vinegar, sugar, capers, olives, pine nuts, garlic, and the tomato paste. Stir and cook about 10 minutes until translucent. Stir into eggplant and chill in refrigerator overnight. Can be served hot or cold.

Lamb Shanks

Ingredients:

4 Lamb Shanks, dusted with flour
Olive Oil
2 cups Red Wine
4 Fresh Tomatoes (or canned)
1 Carrot, chopped
1 Onion, minced
2 tsp. Garlic, chopped
Salt, Thyme, Pepper.

Method:

1. Flour Lamb Shanks and brown in olive oil on all sides. (30 to 40 minutes). Add red wine and water to cover 2/3 of the shanks. Simmer for 1 hour.

2. Add fresh or canned tomatoes, carrot, onion, garlic and spices. Cover and simmer for at least 2 more hours, keep adding water to the pan as needed.

Squash Blossom Frittata

Ingredients:

12 Eggs
1/4 cup Sour Cream
3/4 tsp. Salt
1/4 tsp. Pepper
1 Tbsp. Fresh Oregano
2/3 cup Parmesan Cheese, shaved
12 Squash Blossoms, quarter, sauté in butter

Method:

Sauté the blossoms briefly, about 30 seconds. Remove from pan. Mix, all but blossoms, with a whisk. Pour into a 9" x 13" buttered pan. Top with squash blossoms (cut into quarters) and with chopped fresh herbs and shaved Parmesan. Bake at 350° for 20 to 25 minutes. Cut into squares.

Black Bart Inn, San Andreas, California (2007)

Black Bart Inn & Motel 1927
SAN ANDREAS

*P*resently, the Black Bart Inn's Restaurant has been re-opened. The Inn itself, however, has been converted into offices. Only the motel annex in the rear of the Inn is open. What a shame! As a hotel it had enjoyed an incredible reputation far and wide as one of the hottest places in town for entertainment and dining. During its heyday, when Don Cuneo ran the hotel from 1960-2001, it was *the* place to dine in the Mother Lode.

After all, the name Black Bart alone, elicits the very essence of one of the most exciting eras in Mother Lode history.

The notorious robber of Wells Fargo stages pulled off twenty-eight robberies, but he also wrote poetry which he politely left behind in empty money boxes. The Robin Hood or amiable rogue, whichever you prefer, had the audacity to hang out at police stations in San Francisco, posing as a wealthy business man, displaying a large diamond stick pin, and casually asking questions about the latest Black Bart caper. This man had "style." Part rascal, part Zorro, he created a distinctive role in Western literature, that of the reluctant anti-hero, a highwayman of culture and dramatic showmanship. He contributed to the legends of the West, leaving an indelible memory of a love affair with the dubious Western scoundrel that continues to this day.

I called the Calaveras County Historical Society in San Andreas located in the old 1876 courthouse across from the Black Bart Inn, which houses both the museum and historical society. I spoke with historian Cate Culver. When I arrived, I learned that a large dinner for 150 people was scheduled that evening celebrating the discovery of an original document relating to none other than Black Bart and his capture by a Wells Fargo employee. The guest of honor at the dinner was 89 year-old great-grandson of Reason McConnell, the stagecoach driver of the last hold up by Black Bart.

In spite of the flurry of activity, Cate had taken the time from a very hectic schedule to contact former Black Bart waitress, Gayle Nordby, who had worked at the inn and asked her to share her stories with me. What an afternoon—history in the making! Gayle explained that when she worked at the inn, all of the waitresses had to dress in old-fashioned turn-of-the-century clothes. The restaurant, seating over fifty people, a lounge, a bar and coffee shop were all open seven days a week. And, Gayle added, back then the place was always packed. Besides the fancy clothes, the dishes served in the kitchen were pretty fancy as well. Gayle especially enjoyed the flaming dishes carried down the aisles to the tables. There was Fried Cream with lots of brandy, Cherries Jubilee with vodka, Flaming Duck and much more. Dinners were seven course meals beginning with hors d'oeuvres, relish trays, homemade bread served piping hot with a selection of soups, salads, the main course, and dessert. And these were not small servings, Gayle recounted. There were typically three kinds of steak, and a large array of seafood, from lobster, shrimp, mussels and clams to a wide range of other fish brought in fresh daily from Stockton. One of the most popular dishes was a thick soup called Cioppino. It was loaded with clams, mussels and shrimp simmered in a rich tomato base. The smell, Gayle said, was to die for. The raviolis, Gayle continued, holding up her fingers, were at least five or six inches long, made fresh daily by a local resident. One evening, Gayle remembered, there were several friends who had gotten together for a good time. It was apparent that everyone had a little too much to drink. After they ordered the Cioppino, they began tossing the shells over their shoulders, landing in various places all over the floor and the clean white tablecloths!

Accompanying all of these sumptuous meals was a band which played on weekends and there was dancing. This took place in the "Cave" where the walls were made of solid bedrock, and candles were lit on all the tables. This room was also used for banquets, weddings, Christmas parties and company events. Besides doing all of the cooking, Don Cuneo often staged plays. He was, as Gayle explained, a strong supporter of the arts. During his time, there were lots of famous visitors and movie stars like Randolph Scott and John Wayne.

After this mouth-watering, eye-pleasing description, it was somewhat sad to look out of the window of the historical society and see the large sign, Black Bart Inn—closed. When my interview with Gayle was finished I walked over to the inn. Peaking in the window, I saw a bar which I learned had been in the original lobby. Next door, occupied now by private offices, was the original inn. I wandered upstairs to get a flavor of what it must have looked like "once upon a time."

Reading through the material at the historical society, I learned that before the Black Bart Inn and Restaurant began its life in San Andreas, there was a grocery store on the site. Across the street on the north was the Metropolitan Hotel, built in 1858, that had served the public for sixty-eight years. This was the hotel where Judge Gottschalk declared that the jumping frog story by Mark Twain actually occurred.[1] There were other hotels: The Kinderhook, the Occidental, the Colombo and the North American Hotel.

When the Metropolitan Hotel burned in 1926, the owners announced that they would not rebuild. That's when Bill Treat, an early-day pioneer of San Andreas, decided to build a hotel on top of the old grocery store which faced the courthouse and on its north side, the Metropolitan. At a cost of $45,000, the new and very posh twenty-eight room Treat Hotel had its grand opening in November 1930.

Treat Hotel, San Andreas, California (circa 1930)

Bill Hamby bought the hotel in 1946 and he ran it until 1960 when Don Cuneo operated it up to 2001. In 1983 an annex was added to the hotel, bringing the number of rooms to a total of sixty-five: forty in the motel, twenty-five in the historic hotel. It was at this time the name of the hotel was changed to

[1] According to Cate Culver, Mark Twain no doubt heard the frog story at the Angels Hotel in Angels Camp, but the actual frog jump of old Dan'l Webster may have occurred in San Andreas.

The Black Bart Inn. In 2001 attorney, Ken Foley, purchased it.

Today the historic inn is no longer operating as a hotel, but the motel and the restaurant at the inn are open. The restaurant is now presided over by Chef Kelly Hogge. Don Cuneo still returns to prepare dinners for special events such as the Calaveras Frog Jump weekend and banquets in their banquet room. The newly-restored, historic Red Brick Saloon across the street is also currently open. What are the future plans for the inn? Rumor is that Mr. Foley hopes to restore the inn or possibly interest a franchise buyer in its purchase.

For more information on the Black Bart Inn & Motel, call: (209) 754-3808; Red Brick Saloon (209) 754-9115

Website: www.blackbartinn.com

Location/Mail: Black Bart Inn & Motel, 55 W. Saint Charles St., San Andreas, CA 95249
Red Brick Saloon, 6 North Main Street, San Andreas

How to get there:

From the west on Highway 99, exit State Highway 26 east of Stockton. Stay on Highway 26 and continue east on Highway 12. Take Highway 49 to San Andreas.

From Sonora, take Highway 49 north to San Andreas located between Angels Camp and Jackson.

> Note: In spite of the inn itself being closed, I prevailed upon Don Cuneo to part with the following two recipes...

Apricot Ginger Chicken

Ingredients:

8 pieces Chicken Parts: breast, leg, etc.
2 8 oz. cans Apricot Halves (retain syrup)
2 Tbsp. Brown Sugar
1 Tbsp. Curry
1 tsp. Fresh Ginger, grated
1 tsp. Cornstarch

Method:

1. Roast or fry chicken parts and lay aside.
2. Drain apricot syrup into a small pan. Add brown sugar, curry and ginger. Bring it to a boil.
3. Add cornstarch mixed with a little water. Simmer a few minutes.
4. Place chicken on a platter and arrange apricot halves around plate. Gently pour apricot syrup mixture over the top and serve.

Linguine with Clams

Ingredients:

12 oz. Linguine
3 Cloves Garlic, finely chopped
2 Tbsp. Extra Virgin Olive Oil
1/2 cube Butter
1/2 cup Cream
2 cans of minced Clams
2 Tbsp. Fresh Parsley, minced
1/2 cup Parmesan Cheese, grated

Method:

1. Cook Linguine al dente.
2. Sauté garlic in oil and butter in a small pan. Add clams and cream Toss with Linguine and stir in parsley and cheese. Season with salt and pepper. Serve with French Bread and White Wine.

The Hotel Léger's front entrance

The Hotel Léger in Mokelumne Hill, California

The Léger Hotel 1851

(pronounced "luh zhay")

MOKELUMNE HILL

I had driven along Highway 49 dozens of times between San Andreas and Jackson, but had only managed to
steal a furtive glance at the enticing three-story yellow
Léger Hotel as I sped past Mokelumne Hill.

The day I finally turned off Highway 49 onto the historic
street that led to town, I soon realized that I had arrived at an
inauspicious moment. A wedding was in progress and over 150
guests were descending upon the hotel. The little community
was virtually bursting at the seams. I parked blocks away and

slowly walked through town.

Mokelumne Hill is a place, I discovered, that should be savored slowly. Every structure must be taken in lovingly, because it can transport you into another world, if you let it— a world that time seems to have forgotten. There are no modern buildings of concrete nor neon-lighted strip malls, no parking meters, no stop signs and no mega-chains. "Moke Hill," as locals affectionately call it, has miraculously survived into the 21st century with most of its original Gold Rush charm intact. But whether you stroll or drive down the residential streets, every feature your eyes light upon is an original, shaded by huge overhanging elms, romantically enticing you to drop the cares of the day and stay awhile.

Most people have a hard time pronouncing Mokelumne, including myself. Once I learned that it rhymed with Tuolumne, (both Miwok Indian names), I overcame my trepidation. It was Father Narciso Duran who first recorded the name in 1817 as Muquelumnes. Later, anthropologist Arthur Kroeber, renown as the man who "discovered" Ishi, said the name was derived from the nearby river, or the indigenous people of Mokel. But it would be John C. Fremont who wrote it as we have come to spell it today—Mokelumne—and that spelling has remained.

According to an historic marker a few steps from the hotel, I learned that the hill's first visitors were French trappers in 1848 followed by Colonel Jonathan D. Stevenson of the United States Army Regiment, who was the first man to discover gold here. However, other historic sources I read, credit Samuel Pearsall, a Mexican war hero from Stevenson's regiment, as being the first person to find the sparkling yellow nuggets that changed the world. Colonel Stevenson would go on to prepare a code of laws regarding regulations miners should follow. He wisely foresaw what might happen when eager seekers of their fortunes ran into disputes over claims. And it was none too soon. When the area became the center of the richest placer mining section of Calaveras County, producing over thirty million in gold, his code would have lasting importance.

Like many other gold towns, lots of hooligans merged into the magnet created by the news of gold strikes. A host of the meanest and biggest men flocked to the bonanza. In the year 1851, the town boasted of having killed seventeen people in seventeen weeks and five were killed in one week. When a twenty-four pound nugget of gold was found, an avalanche of miners descended upon "the Hill" and the population rose to 10,000 people. Overnight stage lines ran from Mokelumne Hill to Stockton, Sonora, Jackson, Sutter Creek and a dozen other Gold Rush communities.

With the arrival of so many French gold seekers, Les Fourcahes or French Hill became known as a French settlement, culminating in a "French" war for possession of the gold mines in 1851. Between 1848 to 1854, "the Hill" would boast of having French, Jewish, Irish, Spanish, Chileans, Chinese, Italians, Mexicans and Negroes—a sprinkling of the world's diverse nationalities.

Into this whirlpool of activity stepped George Léger, a suave German born gentleman who claimed French descent. By the time Léger arrived, French merchants had congregated along Lafayette Street, named in honor of one of the American Revolution's greatest heroes, French general the Marquis de Lafayette. Léger became partners with several other men and built his hotel in 1851 or 1852, known as the Hotel d' France. That early hotel was probably not much more than a tent or possibly a wooden frame structure on Main Street. What eventually became the Hotel Léger in 1875 was a combination of three structures, built in three different stages and erected at separate times. These included the old courthouse, an annex and the hotel.[1]

George wanted to let people know that his hotel had class and elegance, catering to the largely European clientele. In time, the hotel helped smooth out the wild and worldly-rough edges of the fandango houses and rowdy saloons which slowly gave way to a more respectable atmosphere and quality of life.

The Léger Hotel was the first building to have electric

---

[1]Larry Cenotto clarifies that complex history in his book, *Logan's Alley, Amador County Yesterdays in Picture and Prose,* Vol. IV., 2003.

lights furnished by another Frenchman, Prince André Ponia-towski and the company he founded, the Blue Lakes Water Company. The hotel was also the first to have a telephone line installed. Later a dance floor was added in addition to a lively bar, and The Léger became *the* place to stay in the Mother Lode.

Three times fires raced through the town—in 1854, 1862 and 1874. The Léger survived the first two, but in 1874, it suffered a $50,000 loss. Just one year later, the hotel was res-urrected with a celebration culminating in a gala ball, in which over 100 carriages pulled up to the entrance. George Léger died just four years later, leaving a legacy which survives today. Indeed, The Léger boasts of being the best place to stay, the best night spot, the best place to dance, play pool and it serves up the best mixed drinks around—especially Martinis.

I wanted to discover all of this for myself, so I made my way through the large banquet hall, decorated with streaming white banners overhead, waiting for the reception of the newlywed bride and groom and their guests.

Jane Canty, one of The Léger's owners was, in spite of her busy schedule, kind enough to take me on a tour of the grounds. Behind the hotel were hundreds of white chairs strewn with flowers along the traditional bridal path. What a glorious setting for a wedding! Vows would be said beneath a beautiful gazebo, resting under a 100 year-old orange tree overlooking a beautiful pool. From here I was escorted through some of the hotel's thirteen rooms. There were three suites, which have fire-places and decks, and one which leads to the hotel balcony, fac-ing the main street. All the rooms are antique-laden, and many have private baths or share baths in the adjacent hall.

We strolled through the dining room, (actually two rooms) which can seat fifty people or more. In the front dining area is an 1875 black walnut, maple and laurel wood bar, where many a miner once exchanged tales of a lucky find, or yarns about the once-in-a-lifetime golden nugget that slipped through his hands.

From the large kitchen, Jane took me down into the bowels

of The Léger.

"I wouldn't want you to come here at night," she said. "Nor would I advise closing that door behind you," she added, smiling.

Yes, The Léger has ghosts—dozens of them. Guests swear they have seen George Léger himself, just as he looked in pictures which hang around the hotel. Jane says that when she enters George Léger's old domicile, the rocking chair just rocks back and forth, as if someone had just gotten out of it—or as if he is still sitting there rocking. Others claim they can hear the mooing of cattle through town on the long cattle drives with their cow bells still ringing. Stories abound. Everyone who has stayed at the hotel has one or two yarns to tell you.

The owners decided to call in Dagmar Morrow, a medium, who accompanied a group of "ghostbusters" through the hotel. They found drunken men in the dungeon, heard George discuss his future projects and other close encounters of the extraordinary kind. You can read about these and more in the nearby bookstore and library adjacent to the hotel.

The dungeon Jane and I descended into has an original dirt floor and massive wooden beams which date from the earliest period of the hotel. Here one can still see the old jury chairs from the original courthouse built in 1851. Today it is used for storage, and many a winemaker has had dinner in its cool recesses, ghost or no.

There are also stories of the locals, both from the old-timers and young-timers who have lived on "the Hill." I met one of them, Mark Borchin, a fifth-generation "Moke." He told me, a green-behind-the-ears newcomer to the Mother Lode, about the many colorful residents such as T-Bone and Cat Fish and Harry.

The story goes that Harry was more or less a dropout from that fast and noisy city to the south who lived, it was rumored, in Marina Del Rey. After a nasty divorce, disillusioned and tired of life in the fast lane, he touched down at the end of China Gulch and East Center Street in Mokelumne Hill. There was once an old Chrysler Station located there in the 1960s,

151

long gone, but he still refers to it as if it were still there. "Going down to the Chrysler building," he tells everyone.

T-Bone was another "intelligent" derelict who had a habit of talking to himself and on any day in town you'll find him dishing out advice from his frequent residency in the center of town, in front of what was once Peek Inn.

As for Cat Fish, Mark continued, he's just a local painter and musician. But these men are what make small towns in the Mother Lode irrepressibly charming and give us all somewhat of a taste of the world they left behind.

Mark also mentioned the catacombs. Closed for years, they were, at one time, tunnels that went under the street. One couldn't tell who was going where, but they provided, in other words, a nice get-away when it was necessary.

The hotel was purchased in 2002 by Ron and Jane Canty, Ron Pitner and Jane's daughter, Ashley, making it a true family affair. Two chefs serve up the best meals in town. Rhiannon Halford is a graduate of the San Francisco Culinary Academy and has worked in the best establishments in Sonoma Valley. With her is Clayton Majors, a local boy, who is attending culinary classes at Columbia College.

For more information, call The Léger: (209) 286-1401
Reservations recommended for the restaurant.

Location: 8304 Main St., Mokelumne Hill, CA 95245

Web Page: www.hotelleger.com
E mail: hotelleger@aol.com

How to Get There:

From the west on Highway 99, take State Highway 26 east of Stockton. Stay on 26 and continue east to Highway 49 to the town of Mokelumne Hill.

From Sonora, take Highway 49 north through Angels Camp and San Andreas to Mokelumne Hill.

Recipes from The Léger

Trout Léger
with Orange Gorgonzola Sauce (below)

Orange Gorgonzola Sauce

Sauce Ingredients:

> 4 Tbsp. Unsalted Butter
> 2 Tbsp. Shallots, finely chopped
> 3 Tbsp. Flour
> 2 cups Heavy Cream
> 1/2 cup Dry White Wine
> 1 Orange, squeeze the juice from the orange
> 1 1/2 cups crumbled Gorgonzola Cheese
> Sea Salt and White Pepper to taste

Method:

Melt unsalted butter, add finely chopped shallots, and cook 'til soft. Add flour to make roux and begin adding 2 cups of heavy cream slowly to pan. Keep heat on low and stirring until mixture is the right consistency. Slowly add 1/2 cup dry white wine and the juice of one freshly squeezed orange. Slowly add in the crumbled Gorgonzola. Add white pepper to taste, a splash of sea salt.

Trout recipe follows...

Trout Léger

Ingredients:

One fresh Trout, whole, cleaned
Flour with Salt & Pepper added for breading
3 Tbsp. Extra Virgin Olive Oil
1 Tbsp. Unsalted Butter
2 Tbsp. Lightly Roasted Garlic, finely chopped
Dry White Wine
1 Orange, slice into wheels
Almonds, sautéed and finely chopped
Dash of Dill and Paprika
Italian Parsley, finely chopped (save some unchopped)

Method:

Coat fresh trout on all sides with flour, salt and pepper. Add extra virgin olive oil and unsalted butter to pan and sear both sides of trout in hot oil and butter. Cook about 4 to 5 minutes per side depending on size of fish. Before taking fish from pan, add the finely chopped roasted garlic and a generous splash of dry white wine, coat the fish with the mixture.

To serve:
Place whole fish on a plate, and set two orange wheels inside the fish. Pour Gorgonzola Sauce over the fish, sprinkle sautéed almonds over sauce, add a dash of dill and dash of paprika, sprinkle with finely chopped flat leaf parsley, parsley sprig on side.

Note: In the courtyard behind the hotel are three very large, very old Orange trees. It has been told that they survived the fire of 1874. Over the years, many owners, cooks, gardeners, have tried to figure out what to do with all those messy oranges. Well, since acquiring the historic Inn, Restaurant and Bar, we decided to use the darn things and dwell upon the many fine things a l'Orange.

—Jane Canty

Painting courtesy of The Léger

Chef Léger and his playmates

"What's on the menu today?"

George Léger's Grand Marnier Orange Sauce
To be used on tarts, tortes, cakes, ice cream and the like

Ingredients:

 1 1/2 Tbsp. Fresh Orange Rind, grated
 1 cup Fresh Squeezed Orange Juice
 1 1/2 Tbsp. Cornstarch
 2 Tbsp. Unsalted Butter, melted
 1/4 cup Sugar
 1/4 cup Grand Marnier

Method:

Whisk 1 cup of fresh squeezed orange juice with cornstarch. Melt unsalted butter in a pan over medium, high heat. Then whisk in sugar, grated orange rind and orange juice until mixture boils and thickens. Add Grand Marnier, lightly simmer, cool. Pour over your choice of dessert. Top with Grand Marnier Cream, if desired.

Grand Marnier Cream

 1 cup chilled Heavy Whipping Cream
 1 Tbsp. Powdered Sugar
 2 Tbsp. Grand Marnier or Cointreau

Whip cream, adding powdered sugar and Grand Marnier slowly. *Viola!*

Drawing by Lloyd Morgan

The National Hotel 1862
JACKSON

*A*s early as 1849, a building stood on the site of today's National Hotel. Mr. Ellis Evans, hailed from Pennsylvania, came west to seek his fortune. He and a partner, a Mr. D.C. White, joined forces and opened a grocery and general merchandise store in 1851 on the site. In 1852 the crude structure burned and a more substantial wooden building took its place: The Louisiana Hotel and Store. The U.S. mail stagecoach regularly stopped at the hotel and made it their stage office.

In 1856 advertising in the local newspaper, *The Amador Ledger,* claimed that their hotel had been thoroughly renovated by its proprietors, Mr. and Mrs. Smith. Those were the days when people chose names for buildings based on their homes back east or in the south and titled their companies after their home states.

During the 1860s as trouble between the North and South escalated, names like the Union and the National were chosen to lay claim to the side they favored both in philosophy and temperament. Someone could always find lodgings at a Union Hotel or the Louisiana.

In July 1862, a hot wind blew through town and the hotel burned—swept away by the frequent fires that raged through the early wooden buildings. The hotel was resurrected and this time with a new name: The National. A legend was born. A year later, a new three-story brick structure rose from the ashes of the old Louisiana Hotel managed by Mrs. Ellis Evans.

Between 1894-96, the original owners of the hotel died. After running the establishment for forty-four years, an Englishman, Mr. Richard Webb, purchased the hotel. He was not only the new hotel owner but the editor of *The Amador Ledger*.[1] The hotel was enlarged and well advertised. After Mr. Webb, a number of new owners came and went. By the 1960s, the hotel

---

[1] Interview: Larry Cenotto, July 2008. *The Amador Ledger* was founded in 1855. *The Amador Dispatch* was founded in 1860. In 1981 both papers were purchased by the *Sacramento Bee*. The paper is now called the *Ledger Dispatch*.

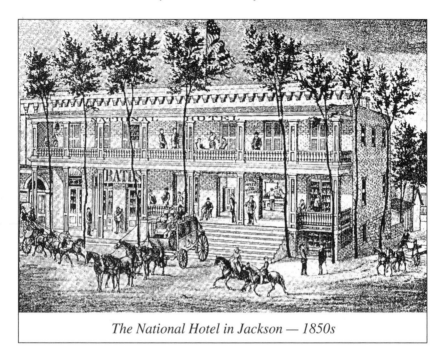

The National Hotel in Jackson — 1850s

was facing demolition. Bernice and Neil Stark purchased it, renovated it and saved the hotel once doomed to be torn down. They brought it back to life, saving her from a fate worse than death—a parking lot. They owned the hotel for twenty-four years. Today, Nancy Banducci and Bill Smith are the angels who run the hotel.

Those are the simple ABCs of the hotel's pedigree. But there is so much more. When film-makers came to Jackson in the 1920s, *The Amador Ledger* ran these headlines: "Movie stars are coming to stage film picture. *Boys Will Be Boys*. Locations to be filmed at the National Hotel." Soon thereafter over forty actors and actresses arrived, causing quite a furor in Jackson, especially when affable star Will Rogers showed up. Everyone wanted to shake the hand of the man America loved.

The community turned out in droves to hear Will Rogers speak, shake his hand and say "aw shucks." Forever the consummate entertainer, Will leased the old Ratto Theater and performed his popular skits for his beloved followers. The audience couldn't get enough of the wit and humor that Will dished out in bucketfuls. Before he left, he handed out ropes to all the small boys in town. The town had not seen so much hoopla ever!

Samuel Goldwyn's company was not the last film company to come to Jackson or to the Mother Lode. It was a popular place to shoot films, especially westerns. And the film stars always stayed at the popular National Hotel. Among the most famous of filmdom's greats were John Wayne and the story of the famous card game that supposedly lasted all night and cost the film legend a mint. Today, you can ask any old time Jacksonian in town what is really their most endearing memory of the town, and it won't be about the gold they found in "them thar hills," it will be about "the Duke." Naturally the story has many renditions, but Larry Cenotto, historian of Amador County, probably has recorded the most accurate.[2]

First of all, the historic poker game took place in February 1963. Director John Ford and "the Duke" and a few of their film sidekicks flew to Sacramento, then drove to Jackson to allegedly look for a filming location for their next movie. They ended up at Tom Rasica's El Pino Club in Pine Grove. When you get five, six or ten groups together, they love to carouse, drink, and play poker and, well—you have the makings of one heck of a night.

The group, so they say, wound up sometime later in Volcano and the small town came out to greet the stars. Then the movie star entourage traveled to Daffodil Hill, Fiddletown, Plymouth and a few other spots, winding up at the National Hotel in Jackson. By the time the guys exited Amador County, Wayne had lost a bundle, ranging anywhere from $2,000 to $50,000 depending on who tells the tale. There arose a disagreement as to the amount Wayne owned and Wayne's agent had to break up the party. One story says that Wayne made out a check for $40,000 signed so illegibly it couldn't be cashed. Another said it was $14,000. A cashier's

---

[2]See Larry Cenotto, *Logan's Alley, Amador County Yesterdays in Picture and Prose,* Vol. IV., 2003.

check, another said, and the amount was $2,000. Take your pick. Whatever the final amount, somewhere in town every year, there are Wayne look-alikes who play the famous screen idol in person, including his famous drawl.

In addition to the dozens of film stars who have visited Jackson, there were other notables: financier Hetty Green, Leland Stanford, Presidents Ulysses S. Grant, James Garfield and Herbert Hoover, royalty Prince Paul of Yugoslavia, Le Count A. Rothschild, Professor Longfellow, Lord Byron, and even Black Bart is rumored to have spent the night.

The day I visited, I spoke to Joan Fox, the bookkeeper for the hotel. I asked her for stories about the hotel and if there are ghosts. "Yes," she said. On the 3rd floor, a Mrs. Bicini has roamed occasionally since the early 1900s. Also Mrs. Fox told me of a very famous madam who had her establishment down the street, Lena's House. There is even a street named after her. She was well-liked in the community, Joan explained. These women ran (for the time) a "respectable business" and the town regarded them differently than they do today.

"For example," Joan continued, "one of the hotel employees was making a delivery to Lena's and who walks out the back door but the Mayor. It was very "hush-hush" and nary a soul mentioned the event." In any case, in the 1950s Governor Edmund "Pat" Brown closed down all the houses of ill-repute, so Lena and her working women had to go.

I asked Joan if there was once a restaurant in the hotel, and yes, there was many years ago, but it is no longer operating. The National Hotel now serves only lunch at the bar.

For more information, call the National Hotel (Jackson):
(209) 223-0500; Fax (209) 223-4845

Location & Mail: 2 Water St., Jackson, CA 95642

How to get there:

From most of California — Sacramento, San Francisco and points north, south and west:

Take Highway 88 out of the Stockton area, east to Highway 49/88. Go south (right) on Highway 49/88 to Jackson. Turn east following Highway 88 and make an immediate left into historic downtown Jackson. The hotel is on Water Street.

St. George Hotel in Volcano, California. 2007

St. George Hotel 1862
VOLCANO

*T*his is the hotel that started it all. In 2004 I was on my way to Daffodil Hill for a book signing and I had to go through Volcano. It was my first jaunt over Highway 88, so the experience was new to me. As soon as I made the turnoff to Volcano past Pine Grove, the entire landscape changed. I immediately thought of the description of Manderley in Daphne du Maurier's book *Rebecca*:

"The drive wound away in front of me, twisting and turning. Nature had come into her own, and little by little in her stealthy insidious way had encroached upon the drive with long tenacious fingers."[1]

---

[1] Daphne du Maurier, <u>Rebecca</u>, HarperCollins Publishers, Inc, Copyright 1938.

Suddenly the St. George Hotel appeared in front of me, an imposing three-story white building that seemed to fly off the pages of Rebecca's intriguing romantic novel. At first the hotel startled me, it seem to come out of nowhere, around a curve in the road, like a small Manderley, jutting out from the huge trees that embraced it. I formed an immediate attachment then and there before I had even entered the front door. I made my mind up that I had to write about this—one more chapter in *Oysters on the Half Shell* began to take shape.

I was able to return to the hotel many times since that first visit in 2004. In fact, a girlfriend and I had our Thanksgiving dinner there. One buffet table was lined with an extraordinary display of hors d'oeuvres, another with the main course, turkey and roast beef, another with salads, and yet another with desserts. The food was ambrosia—fit for the gods. I returned indulgently again and again for seconds and thirds.

By this time I had talked about the hotel so much I convinced my friends that on my birthday, this is the place I wanted to visit. And this time, I wanted to take the time to stop at Black Chasm Cavern, just minutes from the hotel. It is located just off the highway and well worth the experience to see one of the many famous caves in the area. It is one of our latest National Natural Landmarks, and their newest showcave opened in 2000. Visitors are treated to a fifty-minute guided walking tour which displays a colossal room, a platform which hangs seventy feet above a crystal clear lake below. Quite an adventure.

Another attraction, in nearby Pine Grove, is Indian Grinding Rock State Historic Park. If you want to get a better perspective of the Miwok and other native Indians who were the region's first residents, it's not to be missed.

We arrived at the hotel on a quiet, early Monday morning. The lobby, just off to the right as you enter, has the feel of a lodge. There is a huge stone fireplace, and the original wooden floors are slightly uneven which gives one the feeling that you are walking where others have trod for 145 years. There are several comfortable sofas and a very large oil painting of the hotel done by Marianne Weston in 1980.

From the dining room, one enters Whiskey Flat Saloon, built in 1930, which is dark, weathered and funky. Stools and tables are scattered about amid a panoply of paraphernalia collected over the last seventy-five years. One could almost expect Gary Cooper to saunter in and "wolf down" a few drinks before coming to terms with the local sheriff. Dollar bills hang from the ceiling, a large stuffed deer stared at us from over the bar—a red garter draped from one of his antlers and large cow bells dangled around his neck. A weathered harness from the 1900s hung above the door to the saloon and a sign from one of the old streets called Wicked Witch Way was displayed. Old guns and playing cards were tacked all over the walls, relics of past visitors who wanted to leave some small token of their visit to Volcano.

When I asked the owner, Richard Winter, how old the Saloon was he told me it was listed in *GQ* magazine as one of the ten best saloons west of the Mississippi. He added, "Volcano is a town you can walk across in ten minutes." I would venture to say that there are probably more historic buildings per square foot in this small community than any other Gold Rush town.

The Saloon is open for lunch daily, and I sat down with three of my friends to enjoy one of the most scrumptious meals I have ever had. Our waitress recommended a specialty of the house to start with: Pear Cider. Our choices for appetizers were: Vegetable Spring Rolls filled with carrots, cabbage, rice noodles and green peas, served with a sweet and sour dipping sauce. Or we could have Button Mushrooms dipped in a seasoned batter and deep fried to a golden brown, served with a homemade marinara sauce. Or there were Polenta Triangles topped with a creamy mushroom sauce sprinkled with parmesan cheese. Or there was Hummus, which is puréed Chick Peas mixed with garlic, olive oil and cumin, served with pita triangles and olives. And finally homemade Black Bean Chili served with freshly baked cornbread. This was just the beginning. The menu featured a homemade seasonal soup, a house salad, a southwestern Caesar Salad, a

Spinach Salad, Mussels sautéed in a creamy garlic pesto sauce with chopped tomatoes served over linguini, chicken wings, onions rings and steak fries. I had a chicken sandwich. Not the thin-sliced fare usually served, but one large chicken breast so thick I could barely get my mouth around it. My friends chose other things among the appetizers on the menu so that we could all sample everything. The lunch was truly memorable, savory and sublime.

After lunch, Mr. Winter led my friends and I on a magical tour of the three-story,

St. George's beautiful stone fireplace

twenty-room hotel. He described the plans he is making for the future which will make the dining room more private. I asked Richard where most of his guests come from. About 30% who stay overnight are from the Bay Area, he told me, and there is quite an international trade as well. Outside there are upper and lower decks. Each room is decorated individually with lots of antiques. In the summer, musicians perform nightly concerts and there are special events with music, wine, and those scrumptious appetizers.

Outside I was surprised at the commodious acreage the hotel includes. There is a separate garden cottage, a suite with its own kitchenette that has a Jacuzzi tub and a huge shower. Of course there is the old fashioned swing perfect for old fashioned proposals. This seems like the ideal place for them. And there is lots of room for wedding ceremonies among large Magnolias, Coastal Redwoods, Golden Cup Oaks, fir, cedar and Ponderosa Pine trees. One of my friends who accompanied me, Chris Holman, is quite knowledgeable on flora and fauna. She described the special Catalpa tree, which

165

was in full bloom and overlooks the area. There is also a Rose Conference Center which seats up to forty people. The audio visual equipment, Richard Winter tells us proudly, is state of the art. There is also a stage with its own canopy, a place for a full bar and a barbecue. Guests like to spread blankets on the grass and it is wall to wall people when the music gets started. If this is not enough, there is also an annex with six guest rooms named after the old gold mining towns in the Mother Lode. Next to the annex is an outside bar, used a lot during the summer months. And finally, there is even a small gift shop adjacent to the hotel.

Richard showed us the large herb and vegetable garden where the chef can find exactly what he needs for superb dining. The hotel coffee, served every day, comes from Sutter Creek Roasting Company. The meat comes from a local ranch where the beef graze on nearby green hills. My final stroll around the hotel was on the original verandah with a spectacular view of the surrounding trees and hills.

Author leaving the Whiskey Flat Saloon

When I left the hotel, my friends and I wandered around town. We learned that Volcano was discovered in 1848 by Colonel Stevenson who mined Soldier's Gulch in 1849. For a while, the few people who came here called it Soldier's Gulch. That didn't last long. Due

166

to its strange appearance, a crater-like valley, the limestone rock formations, and the morning mist which rises from the valley floor gives it an odd look, reminiscent of a volcano—thus it was named.

In spite of its small size, Volcano has an air of aristocratic elegance and although prospectors were swarming all over the nearby hills, the town became a leading cultural center. By 1855 Volcano boasted seventeen hotels, one of the first lending libraries, a private law school, a debating society, several dance halls, an astronomical observatory site and one of the first theatre groups. By 1858 Volcano had a population of 5,000 and five churches, one public school, a Masonic and Odd Fellows Halls, three butcher shops, two bakeries, two breweries, two express offices, a public hall, a fire company and five saloons

Today, there is still a very active theater group and a prominent amphitheater which brings theater-goers from San Francisco and beyond to enjoy the outdoor productions. As you stroll the one and only Main Street, you should peruse the General Store, today's Country Store, begun in 1852.

None other than A.P. Giannini, founder of the Bank of America, once lived in Volcano. But the town's favorite son is General Liversedge, famous as the Colonel whose regiment ran up the flag on Mt. Suribachi on Iwo Jima in 1944—one of the bloodiest battles fought in the Pacific in World War II. The small gray house, where he was born in 1894, is still intact.

The first hotel on the site of the St. George began as The Eureka in 1853, then the Empire in 1859. Both were destroyed by fire in 1862. When Mr. B.F. George arrived on the scene, he built the three-story building with fourteen-inch thick brick walls and steel shutters to hold at bay the fire dragon. Perhaps that's where the name came from: Saint George and the Dragon.

In the late 1890s the hotel earned the reputation as the best in the county. In 1933 a saloon was added after Prohibition ended. In the 1950s and 1960s, the hotel descended into disrepair and ruin. According to a long-time visitor, only ice cream was served in the summer. The hotel was staring demolition in the face.

That chapter has definitely come to an end. Today the hotel is a sight for sore eyes. I guarantee you that when you leave, you will bid a fond, but sad farewell to the place that has charm by the bucketful.

For more information, call The St George Hotel:
(209) 296-4458; Fax (209) 296-4457.

Location: 16104 Main Street, Volcano, California

Mail: The St. George Hotel, P.O. Box 9, Volcano, CA 95689

E-mail: stgeorge@stgeorgehotel.com

Web Page: www.stgeorgehotel.com

How to get there:

From most of California (Sacramento, San Francisco and points north, south and west):

Take Highway 49 or Highway 88 to Jackson, and then proceed east on Highway 88 for 8 miles to the town of Pine Grove. Turn left on Pine Grove - Volcano Road. Follow Pine Grove - Volcano Road for 3 miles to the town of Volcano.

From South Lake Tahoe, Nevada, and points east:

Take Highway 88 west over Carson Pass, past Kirkwood and Silver Lake to the town of Pine Grove. Turn right on Pine Grove - Volcano Road. Follow Pine Grove - Volcano Road for 3 miles to the town of Volcano.

Recipes from St. George Hotel

Mussels Appetizer (Genovese Inspired)
Serves two

Ingredients:

1 lb. Live Mussels, clean and debearded
1/3 cup Fennel/Anise Bulb, sliced and pre-sautéed
1/4 cup Shallots, thinly sliced
2 tsp. Garlic, minced
1 tsp. Italian Parsley, chopped
1/2 cup Dry White Wine
1/2 cup Fish, Chicken or Vegetable Stock
1 Tbsp. Olive Oil
1 Tbsp. Butter
1/3 cup Tomatoes, (Romas are best, seeded and chopped).
1/3 cup Basil Pesto
Salt and Pepper to taste

Method:

In a large sauté pan on high flame, place mussels, oil, butter, fennel/anise, shallots, garlic, parsley, salt and pepper. Sauté for a few minutes until garlic turns bright white. Then deglaze with white wine. Cook off alcohol for a minute and then add stock and cover with lid. Stir occasionally until all mussels open up. Add pesto and more stock, if needed and stir in thoroughly. Add chopped tomatoes and warm through.

*Enjoy with some crusty French Bread and a
glass of Pinot Grigio or Sangiovese.*

Spring Time Gnocchi

Ingredients:

4 1/2 oz. Gnocchi (Potato Dumplings found in the refrigerated pasta section of the grocery)
1 Tbsp. Olive Oil,
1/2 cup Fresh Asparagus, sliced
1 Medium Portobello Mushroom, char-broiled and sliced.
1/4 cup Red Bell Pepper, julienne
2 tsp. Shallots, diced
1 tsp. Garlic, minced
1 tsp. Fresh Herbs (parsley, sage, rosemary, thyme and oregano)
Pinch Orange Zest
Salt and Pepper to taste
1 1/2 oz. White Wine
3 oz. Vegetable Stock
2 oz. Heavy Cream

Garnish:
1 Tbsp. grated Parmesan Cheese and
6 Pecans, toasted and chopped

Method:

Follow cooking directions on the package of Gnocchi, then pre-heat olive oil in a sauté pan. Add first 9 ingredients and sauté for 2 minutes and then deglaze with white wine. After wine cooks off, add stock and cream and reduce for a minute or two. When sauce becomes thick, present in serving bowl and garnish with Parmesan cheese and toasted pecans.

Southwestern Spiced "Pumpkin" Soup

Ingredients:

1 Butternut Squash, peeled, seeded and cubed
2-3 Potatoes, peeled and cubed
1 Yellow Onion, diced
Olive Oil
1 Clove Garlic, minced
Tomato Purée to taste
6 Cups (or to taste) Stock: Veggie or Chicken Stock
Toasted and Ground Cumin Seed, Coriander Seed and Oregano
Sage
Chipotle Purée to taste
Ancho Chile Purée to taste
Salt and Pepper

Method:

Place the squash and potatoes in a big pot along with the stock and a little bit of garlic with enough water to cover. With a lid on, boil the potatoes and squash 'til cooked. Purée in a blender or one of those hand held things. Meanwhile, sauté the onions and garlic in olive oil along with the spices and herbs over a low flame. When the onions are soft add the squash/potato purée along with the tomato purée.

Add the Ancho and Chipotle to taste. If soup is thick, thin down with more stock. Salt to taste. Simmer for a while so the spices release their tasty goodness and serve piping hot. Throw a garnish on top, preferably something with cilantro, mint or citrus in it.

Volcano Union Inn — 2007

Volcano Union Inn 1880
VOLCANO

*T*here's no question I have "a thing" about Volcano. Partly, because it is the town that initiated the idea for this book. All the Gold Rush communities weave their special charm, but some more than others. Volcano is one of these. You don't have to go searching with guide books in hand for the treasures of the past—you are surrounded by them. The town has changed little in 150 years.

In 1848-49, the men who flocked to California from every part of the world eventually tried their luck here. They descended upon the foothills of the Sierra, a sprinkling of sober-eyed earnest, shrewd, energetic New England businessmen mingled with rollicking sailors, Australian convicts and a few cut throats—a dash of Mexican and frontier desperadoes, backwoodsmen, professional gamblers, whiskey dealers, swindlers and some broken-down merchants, disappointed lovers, black sheep and professional miners. Mix all of these together, season with gold fever, banditos, hard liquor, three-card monte, quarrels, pistols, knives, dancing and gold diggin' and you have something approximating early California society.[1]

Volcano was perhaps more fortunate than some Gold Rush communities. Somewhat off the beaten track, the town survived the loss of her original architectural gems, not only the loss through fire but through neglect and redevelopment.

The old Union Hotel was built in 1880 by French Canadians for the princely sum of $400. There were two other hotels built on the site, but they burned in the 1870s. The hotel site was notorious since it was where the first murder occurred in Amador County. Next door to the hotel was a red house, the residence of Judge Jones who was the presiding judge at the trial. In 2007 the Hedger family owned the home and Matthew Hedger boasts that six children have been born in the house.

The Union Hotel was a boarding house for gold miners run by a Mrs. Murphy who prepared delicious home-cooked meals until 1920. The depression years of the 1930s were difficult, but in the 1950s a revival swept through the Mother Lode. Walt Blomquist re-opened the Union and rebuilt the large stone fireplace in the billiard room with native rocks he found along the nearby creeks and valleys and new life was infused into the old hotel.

The name of the hotel is derived from an era when it was important to make one's allegiance clear during the great Civil War. The Union Hotel was a boarding house for Union soldiers during the Civil War.

Today, Laurie (Hedger) Lockhart owns and operates the eleven-room hotel. She hosts a downstairs tavern that serves pub grub and over 100 kinds of beer, wines and ales from

---

[1]Philip Johnston, "Legends and Landmarks of '49 Along the Mother Lode," *Touring Topics*, 1931, p.12.

around the world. Her guests enjoy their food and beverage of choice while ensconced in a comfortable sofa around a fire, telling a few tales of the way it was "back when."

Volano Union Inn painted by an unknown artist

After most of the gold was removed in the area, (about $65 million dollars worth), it was learned that citizens were tearing up houses and streets in a desperate effort to find more of the shiny metal when times were lean. President Grant signed into law an act prohibiting mining for gold, silver and cinnabar in Volcano, but as a consolation claim, landowners were allowed to build houses on their old claims, hence the name Consolation Street.

The day I visited, the purple mountains surrounding the town were giving way to a bright green expanse of color as the first signs of spring were appearing. Tourists were coming through town in droves, partly because it was close to the special Daffodil Hill celebration when hills above Volcano are simply ablaze with the yellow flowers.

I spoke with Laurie Lockhart and she showed me to the outdoor patio which seats up to sixty. There were originally eleven rooms, now there are four named The Daffodil, The Cape, The Avalon and The Venezia. There is a formal dining room, a parlor and a library. Locals like to walk in, get a glass of beer or wine and browse through the books. There is also a piano which is surrounded many a night with the natives who find solace in sharing some of the old tunes. There is a beautiful fireplace built of native stone by Wolf Blomquist.[2] Laurie told me he only built seven of these in his life and three or four are still standing.

The Volcano Union Inn is a down-home place to stretch one's legs, play pool, have a beer on tap and relax. It is not pretentious—cowboys and bikers feel right at home here.

There is no menu—each day the fare changes and is written on an easel as you walk in. I asked Laurie if you could dance to the songs coming out of the Juke Box. "On the bar, baby," Laurie answered, "if you so desire."

[2]Wolf Blomquist also built the stone fireplace in the St. George Hotel.

For more information, call the Volcano Union Inn:
(209) 296-7711

Location: 21375 Consolation Street in Volcano, California

Web Page, see: www.volcanounioninn.net
  or call the Amador County Visitor's Bureau (209) 223-0350

How to get there:

From most of California (Sacramento, San Francisco and points north, south and west):

Take Highway 49 or Highway 88 to Jackson, and then proceed east on Highway 88 for 8 miles to the town of Pine Grove. Turn left on Pine Grove - Volcano Road. Follow Pine Grove - Volcano Road for 3 miles to the town of Volcano.

From South Lake Tahoe, Nevada, and points east:

Take Highway 88 west over Carson Pass, past Kirkwood and Silver Lake to the town of Pine Grove. Turn right on Pine Grove-Volcano Road. Follow Pine Grove - Volcano Road for 3 miles to the town of Volcano.

Recipes from the Volcano Union Inn

Union Rib-Eye Steak
Serves four

Ingredients:

> 4 Rib-Eye Steaks
> 1 cup Olive Oil
> 1/4 cup Balsamic Vinegar
> 3 Cloves of Garlic, chopped.
> Salt and Freshly Ground Pepper

Preparation:

Mix first three ingredients together and pour over Rib-Eye Steaks. Allow meat to reach room temperature. Add salt and fresh ground pepper over the steak surfaces before grilling.

Bleu Cheese Chicken Salad
Ingredients:

> 2 Large Chicken Breasts
> 1/2 cup Mayonnaise

Continued

1/4 cup Sour Cream
4 Garlic Cloves, finely chopped
3 Ribs of Celery, finely chopped
1 Green Onion, finely chopped
1/2 cup Bleu Cheese, crumbled
1/4 cup Raisins
Salt and Pepper to taste

Preparation:

Poach the chicken breasts. Chill and chop into bite-size pieces. Add the rest of the ingredients and chill. Serve the next day with crackers and fresh grapes.

Asparagus with Chambord Sauce

Ingredients:

One to two bunches Asparagus
1/2 Stick Butter
1 Small Shallot
2 Cloves Garlic
1/4 cup Chambord Liquor (raspberry flavored)
Bleu Cheese
Raspberries
Almonds

Preparation:

1. Steam asparagus until tender, removing tough ends.
2. Sauté butter, shallots and garlic until tender
3. Stir in Chambord Liquor. Allow to gently simmer.
4. Pour over steamed asparagus.
5. Add cool raspberries stuffed with bleu cheese tumbled on top and add a few slivered almonds.

Cinnamon Cream French Toast

Ingredients:

1/4 cup Pancake Mix, (we like to use Krusteaz)
1/4 Tbsp. Cinnamon
1/4 Tbsp. Nutmeg
1/4 Tbsp. Vanilla

Mix the above ingredients into a paste consistency with water.

12 Eggs
1/4 cup Half and Half Cream
French Bread

Preparation:

Beat 12 eggs with half and half until bubbly and creamy and add all the other ingredients together. Use real French Bread, sliced diagonally, and dip the pieces in the egg mixture. Fry in a large skillet until brown, flipping the pieces once.

"*All art is autobiographical;
the pearl is the
oyster's autobiography.*"

Film Director, Federico Fellini
1920-1993

American Exchange Hotel — downtown Sutter Creek in its early days

American Exchange with Adams & Co. Express sign - Sutter Creek, 1850s

American Exchange Hotel 1854
SUTTER CREEK

*J*began my research on *Oysters on the Half Shell* in 2004. My intention was to get an edge on the book while I was completing *Colorful Men, Women & Tales of the Mother Lode*. I discovered, however, that while this approach had some advantages, it also carried some disadvantages. For example, by the time the initial writing of *Colorful Tales* was completed in 2006, many of the hotels I had originally contacted had changed hands, some of the chefs were gone and worse, two of the hotels were closed.

Such was the case when I went back to complete my research on the Black Bart Inn and Motel in San Andreas and the hotel in Sutter Creek.

Sutter Creek is very dear to my heart. My daughter and I always headed for two places in the Mother Lode when she visited. One was Murphys and the other, Sutter Creek. (I had not yet discovered Volcano). The shopping was wonderful, the restaurants superb and there was a decided air of sophistication.

In 2004 as I drove through Sutter Creek, there was a restaurant called Daffodils and above it, an unnamed hotel. I walked inside and found it in some disarray. The restaurant was open, but the hotel was not. The owners seemed vague about future plans, if any, to restore it so I simply removed it from my list.

By 2006 as my research on *Oysters* was winding down, I attended a book signing and was explaining the content of *Oysters* to a local patron, giving him the list of the hotels featured, when he asked me, "Where is the Sutter Creek Hotel?" I explained what I had found two years earlier, and he said the hotel had been recently, beautifully restored and there was a very good Italian restaurant there to boot. A lot can happen in two years!

So, one morning in Jackson, while finishing a television interview program on my new book, I headed for Sutter Creek. Unfortunately, it was 8 a.m. on a Monday morning when I arrived and nary a soul was around. The hotel, however, was impressive and looking through the windows, the restaurant looked splendid as well. Surprise, surprise!

The hotel is called The American Exchange Hotel, which was its original name. The name of their excellent restaurant is Bellotti's. When I returned home, I called the hotel and spoke with Dennis Griffin of Griffin and Associates. Dennis gave me some information, but not enough to satisfy all my questions so I called back a week later. This time I spoke with Louise, an employee of the company. What a virtual storehouse of information! She sent me dozens of long e-mails, and answered most of my questions. All that remained was for me to visit the hotel, look at the rooms and have lunch.

I found that the local *Sutter Creek Gazette* newspaper had

carried some fascinating stories about the hotel in 2006 written by Marv Dealy. The article described the history of the hotel which began when two brothers, James and Samuel Porterfield, arrived from Ohio. The brothers traveled overland in 1849 to strike it rich—not as miners, but by opening a dry goods store. In 1853 the brothers sold their lot on Main Street to Dwight Crandall and Jonathan Jones. Just one year later, construction was begun on the American Exchange Hotel. Why such a name? Because Americans arriving in what was formerly Mexican California wanted to make sure their patrons were aware that the hotel was owned by Americans and they could count on somewhat better accommodations than were possible prior to their arrival.

Under Dwight's supervision the new hotel also served as an office and stage stop for the Adams & Company Express, the very first express company established in California, preceding Wells, Fargo & Company. Three years after Dwight's older brother, Giles, arrived in 1854, the hotel was put up for sale. Finally in 1865, the hotel was sold to M. J. Little and Joseph King for $3,000. Unfortunately, like every other Gold Rush town, fire swept through Sutter Creek in the same year and burned the hotel to the ground. The property was subsequently sold to Albert Rose, who sold it to Lucretia Fifield, later to become the wife of Giles Crandall. Lucretia then turned the property over just months later to her brother, William E. Fifield in 1866. He built a two-story structure that still stands today as the first and second floor of the American Exchange Hotel. On March 23, 1867, the local newspaper, the *Amador Dispatch,* announced that the hotel was open for business.

Many other owners followed. The most significant was Malachi Nixon who bought the hotel in 1895. He remodeled the interior and added a third story with elegantly appointed furnishings. A tradition had begun. Nixon also enlarged the office and dining room to accommodate seventy people and he also operated the old saloon under the name of the Sutter Club.

The hotel stayed pretty much the same until James Bellotti purchased it in 1932. Bellotti first tore down the hotel balcony and then renamed the hotel Bellotti's Inn. He did extensive remodeling, changing what was a forty-seven room hotel into a twenty-nine room facility, adding many private baths. In 2005 the property was sold again to the Griffin Company. They have renovated all twenty-five rooms and brought back the original name of the hotel and restaurant. In 1932 the original balcony had been replaced with an awning. Ugh! In 2005 this was removed and the historic original balcony was put back in place.

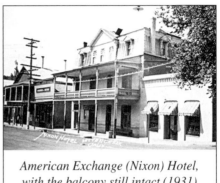

American Exchange (Nixon) Hotel, with the balcony still intact (1931)

Today the twenty-five rooms include two suites on the second floor. A banquet room, which seats up to ninety people, can be reserved for parties, weddings, club meetings and other events.

Bellotti's Inn with the balcony removed (circa 1935)

The hotel rooms have modern conveniences such as flat screen televisions, telephones, wireless internet, many have private baths, and there is a bridal suite. Another nice touch is the fact that all the bathrooms include hair dryers and come with robes and slippers for the added comfort of their guests.

If all this were not

American Exchange Hotel in 2007 The balcony is back!

Hotel Photos courtesy of Louise Reade

enough, there is a gorgeous 1910, 44-note Wurlitzer on display. Guests only have to drop a nickel into the slot (1910 prices) and hear the old masterpieces bring back the musical sounds of an earlier era. During the Christmas season, the mighty Wurlitzer is played a lot.

Through its long history, the hotel has received guests both famous and infamous people as Leland Stanford, Mark Twain, Bret Harte, Black Bart and many more.

For more information, call American Exchange Hotel:
(209) 267-0242; (800) 892-2276.
The inn is open 7 days a week. The restaurant is open Wednesday through Saturday for Lunch and Dinner; a Champagne Brunch is served on Sunday.

Bellotti's Restaurant: (800) 892-2276 or (209) 267-5211

Location: 53 Main Street (Old Highway 49) in Sutter Creek, Calif.

E-mail: louise-reade@thegriffincompany.com

Web Pages: www.americanexchangehotel.com
www.bellottis.com

How to get there:

From most of California—Sacramento, San Francisco and points north, south and west:

From Stockton, take Highway 88 (northeast) past Martell, then turn north on Highway 49 and take Old Highway 49 into Sutter Creek.

From Sacramento take Highway 16 to Drytown and then follow Highway 49 south and take Old Highway 49 into Sutter Creek.

Recipes from Bellotti's Restaurant

Pumpkin Cheesecake with Chocolate Crust

Crust Ingredients:

> 2 Boxes Chocolate Wafer Cookies
> 2 Tbsp. Clarified Butter
> 2 Tbsp. Sugar

Filling Ingredients:

> Four 8 oz. packages Philadelphia® Cream Cheese (softened)
> 1/2 cup Sugar
> 3 Large Eggs
> 1 Tbsp. Vanilla Extract
> 1 tsp. Pumpkin Pie Spice
> 8 oz. (1 small can) Pumpkin Purée

Method:

1. Preheat oven to 325°. In a food processor, pulse the cookies until coarse crumbs. Add sugar and pulse in the clarified butter (not too fine).

2. Press the crust ingredients into a 9-inch spring-form pan.

3. Bake crust for 10 minutes, remove and cool for 10 minutes.

4. While crust is baking, purée the cream cheese and sugar in the food processor.

5. Scrape the sides of the bowl and add pumpkin purée, vanilla and purée 1 minute.

6. Add the eggs one at a time, beating until they are incorporated. Add the pumpkin pie spice seasoning. Pour into cooled crust.

7. Bake at 325° for 35 minutes. (It is done when you lightly shake the pan and it is firm and set).

8. Allow to cool slowly. Remove pan from oven and cool on a wire rack for one hour. Refrigerate 6 hours or longer before serving.

Braised Lamb Shanks

Serves two

Ingredients:

> 4 Domestic Lamb Shanks (the larger the better)
> 2 1/2 cups Flour (divided)
> 1 Tbsp. Brown Sugar
> 1 cup Carrots, diced
> 1 cup Celery, diced
> 1 cup Onion, diced
> 2 cups Beef Stock (or 2 Tbsp. Beef Base and 2 cups water)
> 1 cup Red Wine
> 1/2 cup Olive Oil
> 1 tsp. Fresh Garlic, minced
> 1 Bay Leaf
> 1 tsp. Fresh Thyme, finely chopped
> 4 Tbsp. Melted Butter
> Salt and Pepper to Taste

Method:

1. In a large shallow bowl combine 2 1/4 cups flour (hold the remaining 1/4 cup), salt, pepper and brown sugar.

2. In a 12" frying pan, heat the olive oil to a medium high heat.

3. Rinse the lamb shanks and while still wet coat them with the flour dredge. Place them in the frying pan and cook until flour coating is golden brown. Remove shanks from pan and set aside.

4. With a spatula or wooden spoon, stir any browned bits left in the pan so they don't stick and burn—reduce heat slightly if needed. Next add the carrots, celery and onion to the same pan and sauté until vegetables begin to sweat. Add the garlic, then deglaze the pan with the red wine and simmer for a few minutes reducing the wine only slightly.

5. Add the beef stock, bay leaf and thyme and simmer until the vegetables are just beginning to soften, about 6-8 minutes

Continued

6. Mix in the remaining 1/4 cup flour with the melted butter to form a roux.

7. Stir the roux into the pan a tablespoon at a time to form a thick gravy. Adjust seasoning as needed and remove from heat.

8. Place the four lamb shanks in a suitable baking dish and pour the gravy/vegetable mix over them. Cover with foil and bake in a 350° degree oven for approximately one hour. You will know they are done when the meat pulls back from the end of the shank.

Serve two shanks per plate on a bed of polenta or mashed potatoes and cover with the vegetable gravy.

Chicken Marsala

Serves two

Ingredients:

4 Tbsp. Olive Oil
2 Boneless Skinless Chicken Breasts, 6-7 oz. each
1 tsp. Fresh Garlic, minced
1 Tbsp. Shallots, chopped
1/2 cup Flour
3/4 cup Mushrooms, sliced
2 oz. White Wine
4 oz. Medium Strength Chicken Stock
4 oz. Marsala Wine
1 tsp. Sugar
2 tsp. Parsley, chopped
3 Tbsp. Chilled Butter, cut into 3 slices
Salt and Pepper to Taste

Method:

1. Gently pound the chicken breasts to an even thickness (about 1/4") between 2 sheets of plastic wrap.

2. In a 12" sauté pan, bring the olive oil to a medium high heat.

3. Place flour in a wide shallow bowl and dredge the chicken breasts in the flour, then place in the heated sauté pan.

Continued

188

4. Lightly brown the chicken breasts on both sides. Add the garlic and shallots and deglaze the pan with the white wine. Then add the mushrooms and stock and simmer until the mushrooms and chicken are about 3/4 cooked (about 6 minutes).

5. Turn the chicken and add the Marsala wine, chopped parsley, sugar, salt and pepper. When the liquid is reduced by 3/4 stir in the butter, one slice at a time. This should increase the thickness of the sauce to the desired consistency.

Serve immediately with your favorite rice, potatoes or pasta and vegetables.

Shrimp Linguine
Serves two

Ingredients:

5 Tbsp. Olive Oil
12 Jumbo Prawns, peeled and de-veined, tails on
(recommend 16/20 Black Tiger)
1 Tbsp. Fresh Garlic, minced
6 oz. Dry Linguine
4 Tbsp. Sun-Dried Tomato Pesto
3/4 cup Mushrooms, sliced
3 Roma Tomatoes, cut in wedges
4 oz. White Wine
6 oz. Medium Strength Chicken or Clam Stock
1 tsp. Sugar
2 oz. Grated Pecorino Romano Cheese
2 Tbsp. Fresh Fennel, finely sliced
3 Tbsp. Chilled Butter, cut into 3 slices
Salt and Pepper to taste

Method:

1. In a 4 qt. pot bring 3 quarts of water to a boil. Add 1 Tbsp. olive oil and a pinch of salt. Add the linguine and stir in as it softens. Cook to the desired doneness, drain, and set aside in a bowl and cover to keep warm.

Continued

2. In a 12" sauté pan bring the remaining olive oil to medium high heat. Add the shrimp and sauté until it is lightly seared. Add garlic and stir in with the shrimp. Before the garlic begins to brown deglaze the pan with the white wine and allow to reduce by about 50% as you continue to sauté the shrimp and garlic. Next add the tomato wedges, mushrooms and fennel and sauté until the remainder of the wine is almost completely reduced. Add the stock (chicken or clam) and the sun-dried tomato pesto and stir until an even sauce is achieved. Sauté until the shrimp is fully cooked and the tomatoes and mushrooms are soft. Sprinkle in the sugar, salt and pepper.

3. When the sauce begins to thicken, stir in the butter one slice at a time, this should increase the thickness of the sauce to the desired consistency. Remove from burner and set aside.

4. Arrange pasta on two plates. Remove the shrimp from the sauté pan and briefly set aside. Divide the sauce equally on top of the two plates of pasta and arrange the shrimp on top.

5. Garnish with the Pecorino Romano Cheese and serve immediately.

"*Get action.*
Seize the moment.
Man was never intended
to become an oyster."

President Theodore Roosevelt
1858-1919

The historic Imperial Hotel

Imperial Hotel 1879
AMADOR CITY

*T*he first year my friend, Pat Williams, and I partic-
ipated in Amador City's yearly craft fair, neither one
of us had ever been in this small community before.
Like the hundreds of cars that now rushed past us, we were
either on our way from Sutter Creek, or driving to Placerville.
Amador City was barely a blink along Highway 49. It does
boast, however, of being, perhaps, the smallest incorporated
town in California with a population around 150 residents.

We had chosen a spot to set up our booths over a bridge
which spanned Amador Creek. It was April and the stream was
not yet as full as it would be in June when the snow melted

in the Sierra. On that day it was simply a babbling brook, providing an ideal backdrop for our book signing. The weather was balmy, the tall cedars, elms and cottonwoods swayed slightly in the early morning breeze, and the quaint little community began to wake up, taking on a personality all its own.

It wasn't until mid afternoon that I decided to take a break and stroll through town. I was also famished, not having eaten lunch, so I headed for Andrae's Bakery and Cheese Shop, a bakery that I soon learned deserved the reputation as *the best* bakery in the Mother Lode. Everything is here—a feast for the eye and a joy to the palate.

The small town is nestled in a bend in the road and its businesses and shops are located on either side of Highway 49. The name Amador is derived from José Maria Amador, a Spanish miner and former mayordomo (overseer) from the San José Mission. He was searching for gold. Others came looking for the shiny gold metal, but Amador did not surrender its huge gold lode until many years later when the Keystone and Kennedy Mines were discovered. Meanwhile, a few small shops began to open for business.

The local museum is housed in one of the oldest buildings in town, and there is the old Amador Hotel, begun in 1855, which occupies a large part of the town, now housing a variety of local antique shops. There is the Chichizola Store, a large, imposing structure, begun in 1850 which today contains a shop and a post office.

The building which held my attention, however, was the Imperial Hotel, built in 1879. It began its life as a wooden structure. Its owner, Benjamin Sanguinetti, decided that a mercantile store was needed, but soon changed his mind and decided the town needed a hotel. The hotel with the aristocratic name is, after almost 130 years, surviving well into the 21st century. It fell out of history from 1927 until 1988, succumbing to time and neglect. But Bruce Sherrill and Dale Martin restored it in 1988, giving it a new life.

Today, the Imperial Hotel (Bed & Breakfast Inn) is owned by Mary Ann and Jim McCamant with her son, Tony, and his wife Susan—a family affair. The hotel is a lively, well-known establishment in the Mother Lode, and the food is superb.

Entering the front door, one finds a framed certificate of authenticity that testifies to the fact that professional paranormal phenomenon investigators have gone over the hotel with a fine-toothed comb and found ghosts. They are friendly, of course. Several guests and a pastry chef, among others, have witnessed their presence and testified to that fact.

Visitors are immediately drawn to the hand-carved 1879 Oasis Bar, an inviting and lively part of what is, on Saturday night, packed with thirsty guests. To the right is the Imperial's restaurant, which seats fifty-two people. There is even a special, draped booth for honeymooners or people who prefer more privacy. Large, contemporary paintings by the internationally famed artist, Clayton Pinkerton, hang on the walls next to original antique pieces from the hotel. In back of the hotel is a secluded patio, the stone floor having come from the hotel's original flooring. The gentle sounds of water flowing nearby add serenity and peace. It is shaded by large elm trees. Beyond this patio resides Amador's old city cemetery, dating from the days of '48 and '49 when the first gold seekers arrived.

Upstairs there are six, beautifully furnished rooms, fully air conditioned, each with its own bath and distinct personality. Two of the rooms open up to the outside cantilevered balcony, which gives one a beautiful view of the town's old western charm and entices visitors to stop and smell the daisies.

I sat down with Mary Ann over a bottle of superb Merlot from the hotel's large selection of wines. I explained my book to her and she made a suggestion, which I was embarrassed to admit, I had not thought of myself. First, why don't you get recipes on oysters, since that's the name of your book?" she asked. As a result of that excellent idea I have followed her suggestion and included the hotel's recipe using oysters.

For more information, call Imperial Hotel:
(209) 267-9172.

E-Mail: info@imperialamador.com

Web Pages: www.imperialamador.com

Location: 14202 old Highway 49 in Amador City, Calif.

Mail: Imperial Hotel, P.O. Box 212, Amador City. CA 95601

How to get there:

Take Highway 49 from Placerville south, about 35 miles, through Plymouth. Stay on Highway 49 south towards Sutter Creek and Jackson. About 1-1/2 miles past Drytown, make a left turn onto "old" Highway 49 and go another mile into Amador City.

From Sacramento, take Highway 16 (Power Inn Road/Howe Ave. exit off Hwy 50) toward Jackson. Take Highway 49 south. About 1-1/2 miles past Drytown, make a left turn onto "old" Highway 49 and go another mile into Amador City.

Recipes From Imperial Hotel

Imperial Oyster Stew

Ingredients:

> 1/4 cup Butter
> 2 Carrots, finely chopped
> 1 Stalk Celery, finely chopped
> 1/2 Medium Onion, finely chopped
> 1 pint Shelled Oysters with liquid
> 1 1/2 cups Milk
> 1/2 cup Cream

Continued...

1/2 tsp. Salt
Fresh Ground Black Pepper
Chopped Parsley for garnish

Method:

Sauté the carrots, celery, and onion in the butter until tender. Place in a large saucepan, add remaining ingredients and cook over medium heat until almost boiling. When the oysters have begun to float to the top, the stew is ready to serve. Serve in soup bowls and garnish with chopped parsley.

Mustard-dredged Pork Tenderloin in a Gorgonzola Reduction

Ingredients:

1 Whole Pork Tenderloin (approx. 1/2 to 2 lbs.)
1/4 cup Dijon Mustard
1 cup Heavy Cream
1-2 Tbsps. Gorgonzola Cheese
Canola Oil

Method:

1. Cut pork tenderloin diagonally into approximately twelve 1/4" thick pieces and set aside.

2. Place the cream in a small sauce pan and cook over medium heat, stirring frequently, until reduced by one-half. Add Gorgonzola cheese and continue stirring until cheese has melted and has blended into the cream.

3. Dredge the pork tenderloin slices in the mustard and sauté for 3 to 4 minutes in vegetable oil over high heat. Turn and sauté an additional 2 minutes on second side. Remove from pan and place on a warmed plate. Spoon Gorgonzola reduction over meat and serve with mashed potatoes and sautéed spinach.

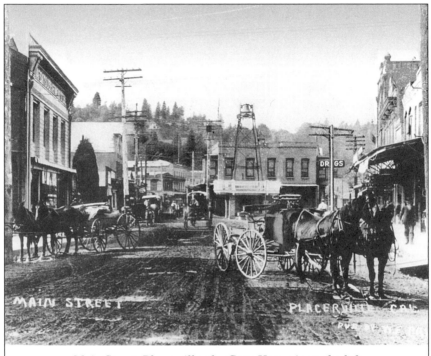

Main Street, Placerville, the Cary House is on the left.

The Cary House Hotel

Cary House Hotel 1857
PLACERVILLE

*I*t has been called the "Jewel of Placerville." Unlike all the other hotels I've listed in *Oysters*, the Cary House Hotel resides in a small city. Placerville is located approximately forty miles east of our state capitol in Sacramento and has a population of about 10,000. It is not only a major hub in the Mother Lode, but continues today as one of the great centers of the central Sierra. Fittingly, it is in El Dorado County, (the gilded one)—one of the original twenty-seven counties in California.

What has always amazed me when I read about the historic

thirst for gold was that it was never satiated. After Hernán Cortés,[1] the Spanish Conquistador, discovered the Aztec Empire in 1519 and ships carried away a king's ransom in gold—the Spanish were still not satisfied. Legends abounded that another rich city further to the north existed—the motherland of all the gold in the world, and they continued to search for it, year after year, decade after decade, century after century. Ironically, just days after the Treaty of Guadalupe Hidalgo was signed, ending the war between the United States and Mexico in 1848, gold was indeed discovered—but not by the Spanish. That feat would be undertaken by an entirely different group of men itching to find their own El Dorado.

On January 24, 1848, at Coloma, James Marshall discovered a small glistening gold nugget along the American River. When the onslaught of men arrived to find their golden dreams, they came in droves over the old Carson Emigrant Road, the main route to Coloma and the awaiting treasure. They forded rivers, climbed the huge barrier of the Sierra Nevada, and found their way to the Sacramento Valley and Sutter's Fort. Along the way, they named the places they had trudged over: Tragedy Springs, Mud Springs, Diamond Springs, Hangtown and a host of other colorful epitaphs.

In 1848 the area, which is now called Placerville, was known as Old Dry Diggins, and later as Hangtown. This title goes to William Daylor, who owned a nearby ranch on the Cosumnes River. Other gold seekers followed, and inevitably, a town was born with parks, streets, overland stages and hotels. By 1854 the town had settled down somewhat after the enormous influx of prospectors and was renamed Placerville. While many of these early hotels have disappeared, the Cary House Hotel, built in 1857 by William Cary, remains.

Boarding houses and hotels were noted for their extravagant menus. Well built roads brought stages loaded with the most exotic food in the world. The Mother Lode was, after all, home to nationalities from all over the world.

One very hot item that people expected to see on every

---

[1]Also known as Hernando Cortez

menu was oysters—oysters for frying, oysters for pies, oysters to gulp down with champagne. Oysters were really a metaphor for the Wild West world of gold-laden California. Up and down the coast and inland, oysters became a symbol of elegance and extravagance, meant to rival anything served on the East Coast. Oysters showed up at the most expensive and swankiest hotels and in the most humble mining towns. The demand for oysters was so overwhelming that the oyster beds in San Francisco were almost wiped out by 1851.

From this hullabaloo came one famous dish: Hangtown Fry. It made its auspicious appearance at the Cary House Hotel. And, of course, there is a story attached to this...

An old miner, loaded down with sacks of gold dust and maybe having had a little too much liquor, was said to have sauntered (reeled?) into the lobby of the Cary House Hotel. He placed his sacks on the counter with a loud bang and demanded that he be served the most expensive dish in the house. He had probably told himself, that if he ever were to strike it rich, he would order the most lavish meal on the menu of the best hotel in town. Those items in the 1850s which were the hardest to find were: eggs, $1 dollar each, and fresh oysters at $6 each. Hearing the demands of the newly-wealthy miner, the chef made up a now famous recipe throwing in some bacon to boot. He called the concoction "Hangtown Fry."

Among Placerville's most famous celebrities is John Studebaker. Leaving South Bend, Indiana in 1853 with a kiss from his mother and $65 in his pocket, he headed for the gold fields. He left behind two brothers who had formed their own firm: H. C. Studebaker, Blacksmiths and Wagon Makers. John, however, had wanderlust so he hoped, like thousands of others, to strike it rich in a golden land. By the time he arrived in Hangtown he had been robbed and worse yet, he found that most of the placer diggings had been mined out. He began making wagons and wheelbarrows in order to keep life and limb together. Finally, in 1858, he left the west with a small fortune of $8,000 and headed back to South Bend, hoping to help his brothers with their wagon business. And well, the rest is history. The firm succeeded beyond their wildest dreams. Studebaker produced over 200,000 automobiles.

In 1912 John decided to return to Placerville for a gala celebration and a huge crowd welcomed their conquering hero. He was a man who had achieved his dreams. Today, in the local museum, one of John's original wheelbarrows is still on display. Unlike many who came west, John held onto his morals and principles, never losing sight of what was really important. His motto was: "Owe no man anything but to love one another."

The three-story Cary House Hotel became the finest hostelry in the gold country—the choice for travelers and the headquarters of Wells, Fargo & Company. Knowing the fate of other structures, this hotel was built as fireproof as possible; it was made of brick. Originally it had seventy-seven rooms and one bath on every floor which had hot and cold running water.

In the early years the Cary House Hotel was a stage stop for travelers throughout the region. It was said that nearly ninety million dollars in gold bullion passed through the hotel from the Mother Lode and from the Nevada silver Comstock Lode. Horace Greeley, whose famous quote, "Go West young man, go West," brought thousands to the golden shores of California.

Originally named after the Cary family, the hotel then passed to the Raffetto family in 1911. In 1915 the building was demolished and rebuilt with the same bricks, giving it a new life and it was re-named the Placerville. Sixteen years later, the name was changed once again and became the Raffles Hotel until 1977, when the Milton family restored the hotel and re-turned it to its original name: the Cary House Hotel.

Today the hotel is the last of the dozens of hotels that once graced Main Street. It is still called "The Belle of Main Street," however, having undergone extensive renovation. The Cedar Room restaurant was eliminated in 1980.

The current owners are aware of the hotel's historic significance and its importance in today's fast-paced society. When I spoke with the hotel's manager, I was told: "What sets us apart from most hotels is our special historic interest. In our remodeling we have made this history visually interesting as well as authentic to maintain the ambiance our guests expect. All the rooms reflect the styles from the 1850s."

The hotel has had its share of famous guests from Mark Twain to President Ulysses S. Grant to Black Bart. More recently, movie stars such as Bette Davis, Reginald Owen, Molly Ringwald, Ed Asner and Brooke Shields enjoyed their stays at the Cary House Hotel.

When I visited, I was impressed that this hotel, among all the others I had seen, was not only the tallest, (four stories) but was the most modern in appearance. The lobby is striking with four large stained glass panels done by a local artist, Wendy Wythe. In front of the glass is a large Grand Piano, brought around Cape Horn at the turn of the 19th century and donated by a prominent family in 1998. The elevator is reputed to be the second oldest west of the Mississippi River.

Today the Cary House Hotel has thirty-eight antique-laden rooms with private baths. No two rooms are the same and each floor has a theme. The Milton Room awaits guests for special occasions such as weddings, receptions, business meetings, corporate retreats, seminars and conferences. Outside is an adjoining courtyard where guests can enjoy a deluxe continental breakfast.

For more information call the Cary House Hotel: (530) 622-4271
E-Mail: manager@caryhouse.com
Web page: www.caryhouse.com
Mail: Cary House Hotel, 300 Main Street, Placerville, CA. 95667

How to get there:

From Sacramento:
Take Highway 50 eastbound to Placerville. Turn right at Hwy. 49 South (2nd stoplight), then turn immediately left onto Main Street. The hotel is about 1 1/2 blocks on the right.

From Lake Tahoe:
Take Hwy. 50 westbound to Placerville. Turn left at Bedford Street (1st stoplight), then turn right onto Main Street. The hotel is about two blocks on the left.

Recipe From The Cary House

The Famous Hangtown Fry

Ingredients:

> 1/2 lb. Bacon
> 6 to 10 Oysters, shucked
> 1 Egg, beaten with a teaspoon milk or cream.
> 6 Eggs
> Soda crackers crumbled
> 4 cups milk or cream
> 1/4 cup Fresh Parsley, chopped
> Freshly grated Parmesan Cheese

Method:

Fry bacon until crisp. Set aside. Pat oysters dry and dip in egg, then coat with cracker crumbs. Saute in cooking oil until almost cooked. In a mixing bowl beat 6 eggs with milk or cream, parsley and cheese, salt and pepper. Pour egg mixture over oysters in the pan, reduce to low heat and scramble the eggs. Place pan under a broiler to brown lightly and transfer to a heated platter and garnish with crumbled bacon and parsley.

To this day, the concoction is still served
(with some variations) worldwide.

"Why then
the world's mine oyster,
Which J
with sword shall open."

William Shakespeare
1564-1616

SPONSORS
Business Directory

(Kindly Support Our Advertisers)

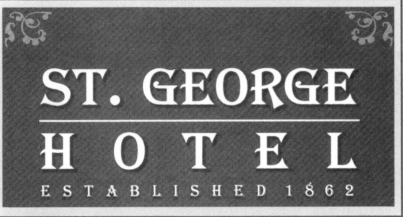

215

"If you don't love life, you can't enjoy an oyster;
there is a shock of freshness to it and intimations
of the ages of man, some piercing intuition
of the sea and all its weeds and breezes.
[They] shiver you for a split second."

American writer, Eleanor Clark
1913-1996

Biography

Janet Atkinson

About the Author

Janet I. Atkinson, a native southern Californian, attended U.C.L.A. and Cal State Northridge with degrees in Art History and History. She has taught classes in Art History, California History and Humanities at Cal State L.A., Glendale College, Pierce College, Columbia College, and Cal State Stanislaus.

She wrote *Los Angeles County Historic Directory* in 1988; followed by *Gold Rush Tales* in 1997; *Colorful Men & Women of the Mother Lode* in 2002 with a second printing in 2004. *Colorful Men, Women & Tales of the Mother Lode* followed in 2006. Janet has written for the *Society of Architectural Historians*, *Los Angeles* magazine, *Elan* magazine, *Treasure, Chispa Historic Quarterly*, *Central Sierra Seasons* magazine and more. Jan was selected by the Sacramento Public Library for *Authors On The Move* 2004-05. She appeared on Jackson television TSPN in 2006. Ms. Atkinson has given talks to clubs, organizations, and many historical societies throughout California.